The Learning Works

Teaching Val[ues]
Reaching Kids

Character Education Activities to Help Teach
Honesty • Respect • Cooperation • Perseverance
Compassion • Responsibility • Courage • Tolerance

Written by Linda Schwartz • Illustrated by Bev Armstrong

The Learning Works

Editing and Text Design:
Clark Editorial & Design

Illustration:
Bev Armstrong

Cover Photograph:
Superstock, Inc.

Copyright © 1997
The Learning Works, Inc.
Santa Barbara, California 93160

ISBN: 0-88160-299-X
LW 369

Printed in the United States of America.

Acknowledgments

Special thanks to Michele Makagon and the teachers at Escalona Elementary School in Norwalk/La Mirada School District for their insights and feedback.

Contents

Contents
continued

Perseverance • 99–124

Contents
continued

Compassion • 125–152

Responsibility • 153–178

Contents
continued

Courage • 179–202

Tolerance • 203–223

To the Teacher

This is a book about values and how to teach them to your students through discussions, role-playing, and writing. Since values differ from culture to culture, the activities have been kept open-ended to encourage a variety of responses and ways of handling each situation.

It is recommended that you feature a different value in your class each month. Create a learning center for the value, design a bulletin board, and send a letter home to your students' parents to make them aware of the value you are covering in class each month. Ask for their support and cooperation in discussing and practicing the value of the month at home.

Many of the values presented overlap each other. For example, if you are discussing cooperation with your students, the values of respect, compassion, and tolerance also come into play. As you and your students get involved in the discussions, role-playing, and writing activities presented throughout this book, be sure to point out how many of these values are interconnected to one another.

Here are some other ways to reinforce the values being taught:

- Create a simple newsletter to send home each month which highlights the things your students have done to demonstrate the value being taught.

- Honor students at an assembly each month and present award certificates to acknowledge those students who have gone out of their way to practice the value being featured.

- Post pictures and write-ups of outstanding students on the office bulletin board.

- Encourage your colleagues to teach this unit on values. Have all classrooms focus on the same value each month and make it a school-wide project for the entire year.

Chapter 1
Honesty

truthfulness; sincerity

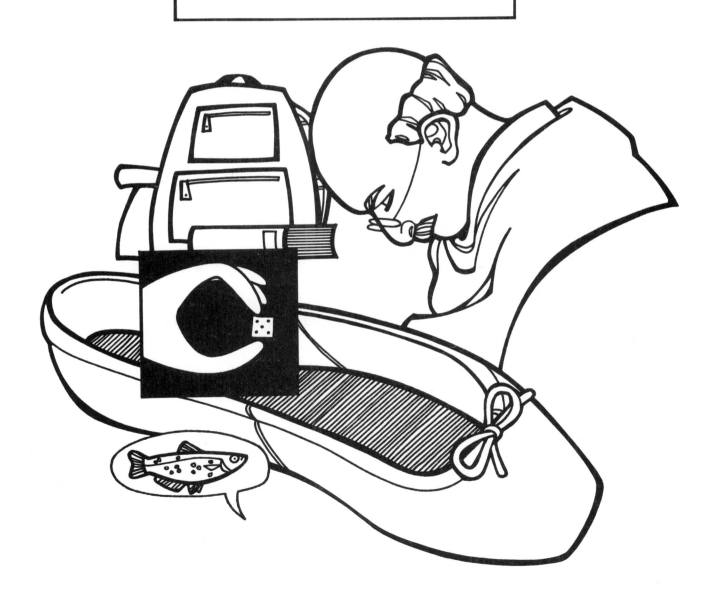

A Letter to Parents

Dear Parents,

This month our class will be learning about the value of **honesty** through discussions, role-playing, creative writing, and art. We will be learning ways to be honest with ourselves and with the other people we come in contact with at home, at school, and in the community.

Whenever possible, please take time to talk to your child about honesty. Children learn more by your actions than your words so continue to set good examples for them to follow. Set up hypothetical situations when you are with your child. Talk about how you would deal honestly with a salesperson giving you too much change, or telling a police officer you were exceeding the speed limit instead of making an excuse or not being honest about the speed you were traveling.

Provide positive reinforcement by complementing and praising your child when he or she handles a situation honestly. If your child tells a lie, take the time to explain how being dishonest not only hurts him or her, but also the other people involved. Help your child set goals regarding honesty, not only for this month but for a lifetime.

Here are other ways you can reinforce the value of honesty with your child:

- Visit your library and read books dealing with honesty as a theme or books about people who have spoken or behaved honestly.

- Watch a video together that deals with honesty.

Thank you for being our partner in helping to teach your child the value of **honesty**. Please feel free to visit our class and see what we're doing to learn more about being honest.

Sincerely,

What is Honesty?

In your own words, describe what the word *honesty* means.

_____

_____

_____

_____

Find the word *honesty* in a dictionary and write its definition below.

_____

_____

_____

_____

Describe a time when you weren't completely honest with a friend or family member. How did you feel about not telling the truth?

_____

_____

_____

_____

Describe a time you were completely honest with someone in a difficult situation.

_____

_____

_____

_____

What Are Ways of Being Honest?

You are being honest when you . . .

- do your own homework instead of copying from a friend

- tell a friend the truth, not just what he or she wants to hear

- explain that the reason you didn't turn your homework in on time was because you didn't budget your time wisely—not because "your dog ate it"

- keep your eyes on your own paper, not your classmate's, during a test

- tell the truth about your age even if it means paying more money to get into a movie

- clean up your room after you make a promise to your parents that you will do it

- give a cashier the extra money she gave you by mistake when making change

- write a report in your own words instead of copying information word-for-word from an encyclopedia or reference book

- admit you made a mistake and not blame others

- keep a friend's secret after you've promised not to gossip or share it with others

- turn in a wallet full of money that you find on the floor of a restaurant

Just for Fun

Draw a cartoon showing someone who is caught being dishonest.

12

Being Honest With Yourself

Before you can be honest with other people, you have to be honest with yourself. Here are some examples of ways you can be honest with yourself:

- Accept responsibility for your own actions; don't blame others.

- Be honest about your feelings. Tell people how you honestly feel, not what you think they want to hear.

- Face issues as they arise. Don't try to avoid tough situations by telling half-truths or white lies.

- If you are considering cheating, lying, or being dishonest, try to think of how it will make you feel in the long run. Will dishonesty solve the problem or just delay it and maybe make it worse?

- When confronted with a situation involving honesty, think about all the ways in which your actions might affect others. What happens if you lie about toilet-papering a neighbor's house and the wrong person is punished? What if you fail to tell a salesperson that she gave you an extra five dollars in change? Will the difference have to come out of her salary?

Thinking About Honesty

When you aren't honest with others, you not only hurt yourself, you hurt other people as well. Discuss each situation and try to see the situation from more than one side. Put yourself in each person's place. Then, on a separate piece of paper, describe how each person would be affected for each scenario.

A fifth-grade girl complains to her mother that her teacher doesn't like her, grades her papers unfairly, and always criticizes her in class. The girl is not being honest. She doesn't pay attention in class, doesn't complete her assignments, and is rude.

How are the following people hurt by the girl's dishonesty:

the girl?
the mother?
the teacher?
the other students in the class?

You are an avid baseball card collector. Your friend's younger brother brings you a valuable card that he wants to trade. Since you are older and more familiar with the value of baseball cards, you know that the card he wants to trade is worth far more than the card he wants from you. You make the trade with him anyway.

Is it up to the boy to know what he's doing? Are you being dishonest by taking advantage of his age and inexperience? How is each person affected by the trade:

you?
the younger child?
your friend?

14

Thinking About Honesty

Tony is an excellent student and is well liked by all his peers. His older brother, however, is a member of a gang and is always in trouble. One day the older brother robs a grocery store. The younger boy knows his brother was involved because he overhears him bragging to some of his buddies. The next day the police come to Tony's house to investigate. They ask Tony what he knows about the robbery. Should he lie to protect his brother or tell the truth because he knows that stealing is dishonest and wrong?

If Tony lies, how are the following people hurt:

Tony?
his brother?
other members of his family?
the other members of the gang?
the owner of the store?
other customers of the store?
the people in Tony's community?

A True Story

On a separate piece of paper, describe a time you were confronted with a situation where you had to choose between being honest or dishonest.

- Tell what other people were involved and what led up to the dilemma.

- Tell how you resolved the situation and how you felt about it afterward.

- Describe what you learned and what you would do differently if the same situation came up again.

- If you feel comfortable doing so, share your story with your classmates. Get their feedback, and listen to their comments. You might be surprised to learn that many classmates have had a similar experience. It will be interesting to see how different people handle similar situations in different ways.

Setting Goals for Yourself

Throughout this book, you will be asked to set goals for yourself as you begin each new chapter and then evaluate yourself at the end of the chapter to see if you have reached your goals. When setting goals for yourself, be sure they are "do-able" and realistic. For example, rather than setting a goal of becoming a concert pianist, a more realistic goal is to practice playing the piano for a half an hour or more three times a week.

On page 17 set three honest, realistic goals for yourself in any of the following areas:

- schoolwork

- health

- afterschool activities

- relationships with friends

- relationships with family members

- your community

For each of the three goals, list the first step you can take to get started.

16

Setting Goals for Yourself
continued

Goal 1

_____

_____

_____

_____

Goal 2

_____

_____

_____

_____

Goal 3

_____

_____

_____

_____

What Are Ways People Are Dishonest?

People can be dishonest in many ways. Here are a few examples:

withholding important information or "lying by silence"

lying to a teacher

exaggerating the truth

lying to protect someone else

cheating in a game

shoplifting

On a separate piece of paper, list ways people might be dishonest to five of the following people or groups of people:

- a brother or sister
- a parent
- a neighbor
- a friend
- a salesperson
- a teacher
- a coach
- a police officer
- a grandparent
- a principal
- a scout leader
- their community
- their state
- their country

Why People Don't Always Tell the Truth

Being honest is not always easy. Many times people lie because it helps them out of a tough situation for the moment. But later they sometimes have to tell another lie to cover the first one they told, which just makes matters worse. Why do people lie?

- **They are afraid to tell the truth because they are afraid of what might happen to them.** Describe a situation where kids your age might not be completely honest because they are afraid to tell the truth.

_____

_____

_____

_____

- **They feel that if they tell the truth, they will hurt someone's feelings.** Describe a situation where someone your age lies to avoid hurting someone's feelings.

_____

_____

_____

_____

- **They feel it is easier to lie than it is to tell the truth.** Describe a situation where someone your age doesn't tell the truth because it is easier and less complicated to tell a "little white lie."

_____

_____

_____

_____

Honesty at Home

Brainstorm with your classmates to make a list of different situations dealing with honesty at home. Here are some examples:

- You are watching your favorite show on television. Your dad asks if you have finished all your homework. You tell him you have even though you haven't started your math and social studies assignments.

- Your grandmother is visiting for the weekend and asks if you want to go shopping with her. You don't want to go. You tell your grandmother you have a lot of homework you need to finish even though you don't have any homework due.

How many other situations can you think of that deal with honesty in the home? Your list should involve all members of your family.

20

Honesty at Home
continued

Look at the list you created from the previous page. As a class, read each situation and discuss how each one could have been handled more honestly. Think about possible compromises that could have been worked out in each situation. In your discussion, consider the following questions:

- Do you think it is ever okay to lie to someone? Why or why not?

- What if, by being completely honest, you hurt someone's feelings? Is it okay to tell a lie or not tell the whole truth to spare someone's feelings?

Role-Playing Honesty at Home

Think about what you would do in each of the following situations. Then role-play the situation with several of your classmates. Show the rest of your class how you would successfully solve each problem.

Your mom asks if you like the new dress she just bought on sale. You don't like the way it looks on her. You think it is the ugliest dress you have ever seen.

You receive a CD for a birthday gift from your aunt. You already have this CD in your collection. Your aunt calls to see how you liked her gift.

A friend asks you to copy your favorite computer program for him. He doesn't want to buy his own copy because he hasn't saved up enough money.

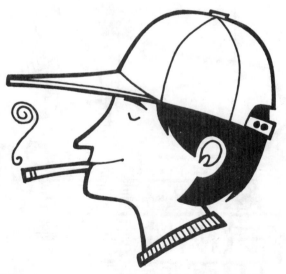

You see your older brother smoking at home. He makes you promise not to say anything to your mom or dad. Later, your mom smells smoke in the room and asks you if someone has been smoking.

Exaggerating

In your own words, tell what the word **exaggerating** means.

_____

_____

_____

_____

Why do you think people exaggerate? _____

_____

_____

_____

Do you think exaggerating is the same as lying? Why or why not? _____

_____

_____

_____

What is wrong with exaggerating? _____

_____

_____

_____

On a separate sheet of paper, describe a time you exaggerated to your mom or dad, to your brother or sister, to a close friend, to a relative, or to a teacher. Describe how you felt while you were doing it. How did you feel later? What did you learn from this experience?

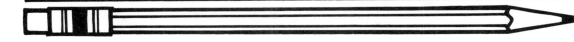

Honesty at School

Brainstorm with your classmates to make a list of different situations involving honesty at school. Here are some examples:

- You haven't studied for an important math test. An hour before the exam, you lie to your teacher, telling her that you have a bad headache and need to go home.

- You go to a ball game instead of reading a chapter and taking notes on a chapter in your science book. You ask a friend to lend you his notes so you can copy them.

- You see a five-dollar bill fall out of someone's pocket on the playground. He or she doesn't realize that the money is missing.

How many other situations can you think of that involve honesty at school? Make a list that includes situations that might occur in the classroom, on the playground, in the cafeteria, or on the way to or from school.

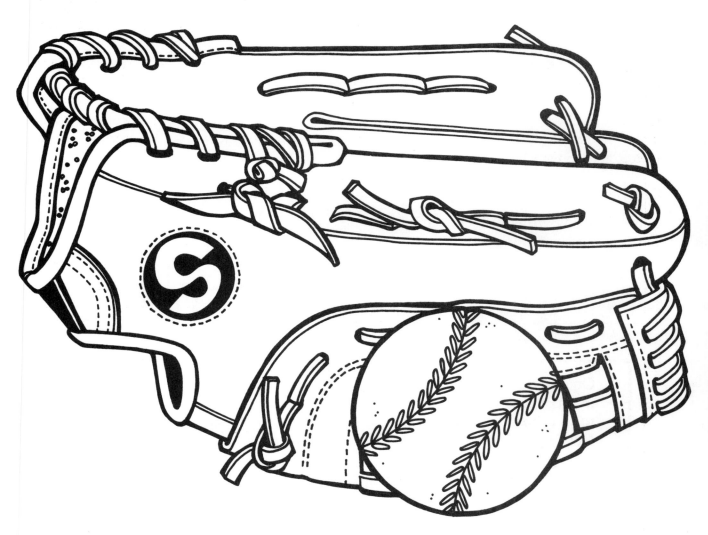

Honesty at School
continued

Look at the list you just created from the previous page. As a class, read each situation and discuss how each one could have been handled more honestly.

Can you remember a time you weren't honest at school? It could have been a situation dealing with your principal, a teacher, an aide, or a classmate. On a separate piece of paper, write about:

- the events leading up to the incident

- the people who were involved

- what actually happened

- what you learned from the experience

- how you would handle the same situation again

This activity if just for your own self-evaluation and growth. You do not have to share it with others unless you choose to do so.

If you have never been dishonest at school, make up a story about someone who is dishonest and how the issue is resolved. In your story, describe what this person learns from the situation.

Did you ever discover that someone at school was not honest with you? Describe what happened and how you felt. How was the situation resolved?

_____

_____

_____

_____

_____

_____

_____

_____

Role-Playing Honesty at School

Think about what you would do in each of the following situations. Then role-play the situation with several of your classmates. Show the rest of your class how you would solve each problem.

You see a fight break out on the school playground after lunch. The aide on duty asks you what happened and who started the fight. Your best friend is the one who started the fight.

You receive an "A" on your social studies final. When you check your score, you discover that your teacher added incorrectly. You should have had a "B" instead. This will lower your report card grade.

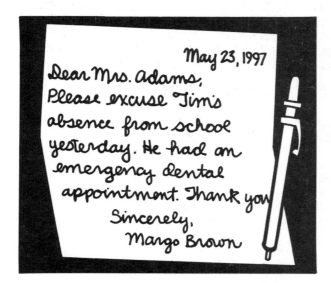

A friend asks you to forge a note explaining his absence from school the previous day.

You forgot to do an important homework assignment. Your teacher asks you why you didn't do the assignment.

A Poem About Honesty

A **cinquain** is a simple poem with five lines. Its structure follows a specific pattern.

Pattern:

line 1—one word of two syllables (may be the title)
line 2—four syllables (describing your subject or title)
line 3—six syllables (showing action)
line 4—eight syllables (expressing a feeling or observation about your subject)
line 5—two syllables (describing or renaming your subject)

Example:

Honest
Being truthful
Telling it like it is
Makes you feel good inside yourself
No lies

On a separate piece of paper, write a cinquain on the subject of honesty or telling the truth. Your cinquain might deal with not stealing or not copying during a test. Follow the pattern described above. Illustrate your cinquain and share it with your classmates.

Read All About It!

Reading Newspaper Articles About Honest People

Newspapers often feature articles about everyday people who do honest things. For example, a person who finds a wallet full of money and credit cards returns the wallet and its contents to its rightful owner.

Here's an activity for your whole class.

- Read your local newspaper for a few weeks and find articles about honest people.

- Cut out the articles out and bring them to school.

- As a class, discuss each article and the options the person faced. How would the results have been different if he or she chose to be dishonest? What other people would have been affected? In what ways?

- Post the articles on a classroom bulletin board. Add to your display as you find other articles about honest things people do for others.

Reading Biographies of Honest People

- Go to your school or local library and find biographies about people who have spoken or behaved honestly, even when doing so was difficult or dangerous. Select one of these books to read.

- After reading the book, write a one-page report highlighting interesting facts about the person's life and the honest things he or she did. Pretend you are the subject of the book, and write your report using the word "I." For example . . .

  Even before I became the sixteenth president of the United States, people called me Honest Abe. Here's an interesting story of how I got my nickname. It all began when . . .

- Present your report to the class, using props and visual aids. If possible, come dressed as the person you selected.

Teaching Values—Reaching Kids
© The Learning Works, Inc.

Read All About It!
continued

Congratulations! You made the headlines for an honest deed you did. Write a newspaper article for your local paper describing your honest act. In your story, answer the five W's—Who? What? When? Where? and Why? Create your own newspaper headline. Draw a picture of yourself in the box and write a caption to go underneath it. Read your story to your classmates.

Create a Story in Pictures

In the real world today, there will always be people who are dishonest—people who cheat on their taxes, people who steal office supplies from their bosses, or people who lie to avoid the consequences of their actions. But there are also many honest people who would never consider being dishonest.

Using illustrations and words, create a story that features one of the situations listed below or make up your own situation. On a separate piece of paper, create your picture story showing how your character resolves the tricky situation in an honest way. Your picture story should have a title and at least six illustrations to develop the action and dialogue. Use cartoon bubbles to show what your characters are saying. Share your picture story with your classmates.

Tricky Situations

- You break your mom's favorite antique vase while wrestling with your brother.

- A classmate always has bad body odor.

- Your aunt wants you to lie about your age so she can get you into an amusement park for a cheaper price

- Your parents forbid you to see a certain movie. You are staying with a friend who wants to go see the movie. Her parents don't care if she sees it.

30

Finish the Story

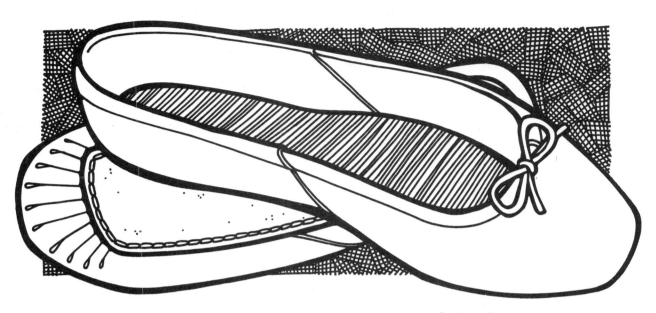

Kate was in deep trouble; she was doing poorly in science. Her grade, just before the big final, was hovering somewhere between a "C–" and a "D." Her parents had warned her that if she didn't bring her grade up to at least a "C" on her next report card, she wasn't going to be able to continue with her ballet lessons. The final exam was tomorrow, and although she had tried hard and studied every night, she still didn't feel confident that she knew the material. But she just had to do well! Ballet was everything to her, and she couldn't imagine not having her ballet lessons to look forward to each week.

After leaving science class, Kate realized that she had left an overdue library book in the room. She ran back to get it. The classroom door was wide open, but her teacher, Ms. Thompson, was nowhere to be seen. She grabbed the library book from her desk and headed for the door when she saw the exam. There, sitting on Ms. Thompson's desk was a copy of the science final with all the answers marked in red pen. Answers to the multiple choice questions, answers to the true-and-false questions, even the three essay questions were right in front of her.

(On a separate piece of paper, finish the story.)

Summing Up Honesty

Complete each statement or question.

Something new I learned about honesty is _____

_____

_____

_____

Did you reach the "honesty" goals you set for yourself? Give examples of how you are moving toward them or have accomplished them.

_____

_____

_____

_____

One area I still need to work on when it comes to honesty is

_____

_____

_____

_____

Quotes on Honesty

- There is no wisdom like frankness.
  Benjamin Disraeli

- I hope I shall always possess firmness and virtue enough to maintain what I consider the most enviable of all titles, the character of an honest man.
  George Washington

- A harmful truth is better than a useful lie.
  Thomas Mann

- To make your children capable of honesty is the beginning of education.
  John Ruskin

- Honesty is the best policy.
  Miguel De Cervantes—from *Don Quixote*

- We must make the world honest before we can honestly say to our children that honesty is the best policy.
  George Bernard Shaw

- Honesty is the first chapter of the book of wisdom.
  Thomas Jefferson

- Examine what is said, not him who speaks.
  Arabian proverb

Quotes on Honesty

- An honest man's word is as good as his bond.
  Cervantes

- If you tell the truth you don't have to remember anything.
  Mark Twain

- A show of a certain amount of honesty is in any profession or business the surest way of growing rich.
  La Bruyere

- A "No" uttered from deepest conviction is better and greater than a "Yes" merely uttered to please, or what is worse, to avoid trouble.
  Mahatma Gandhi

- Honesty is largely a matter of information, of knowing that dishonesty is a mistake.
  Edgar Watson Howe

- No legacy is so rich as honesty.
  William Shakespeare

- One falsehood spoils a thousand truths.
  Ashanti proverb

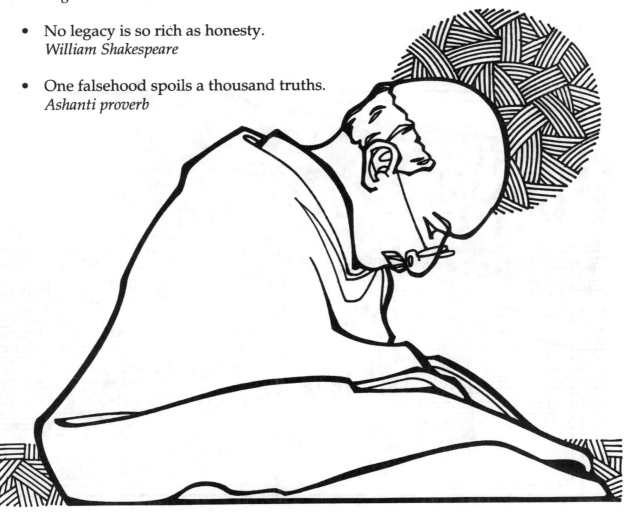

Student Follow-Up Activities
Honesty

- Design a bumper sticker in honor of "Honesty Week."

- As a class, brainstorm a list of synonyms and antonyms for the word **honesty**. For example, under *synonyms*, you might list words such as integrity, honor, and truthfulness. Under *antonyms*, you could list words such as dishonesty, deceitfulness, and deception. Then use these words to create a word search puzzle for other members of your class to solve.

- Read your local newspaper, and look for articles that have to do with people lying, stealing, or cheating. Tell how the problem could have been avoided if people had been honest.

- Design a mural with your classmates that reflects the theme of honesty.

- Create a class bulletin board with famous sayings about honesty.

- Make a classroom display of cartoons that show the consequences of dishonesty.

Student Follow-Up Activities
Honesty

- Write a short skit to perform for younger students that teaches them about honesty at home, at school, or in the community.

- Plan a poster contest. Create original messages and pictures to teach others about honesty. Display your winning posters in the cafeteria or school office.

- Write about a time you weren't honest with an adult—other than a family member. What were the short-term and long-term consequences of your actions? What did you learn from the experience?

- Look for examples of how honesty or dishonesty is portrayed in the television shows you watch for a period of one week. Make a list of these incidents and use them as a focal point for discussions with your classmates.

Teacher Follow-Up Activities
Honesty

- Create an "Honesty Week" in your class. Have each student try to do at least three honest things each day for another student, adult, family member, or person in your community. As a class, make a list of all the honest things you do.

- Sometimes it takes courage to be honest. Have students share incidents where they chose to be honest in a difficult situation. Discuss other alternatives they could have taken and how that would have affected everyone involved.

- Discuss the concept of "the little white lie." Ask students to give examples of white lies they have either told or heard. Then discuss the consequences of telling white lies and brainstorm alternative solutions to each of the examples they bring up in your discussion.

- Have a classroom discussion on "white lies" students have discovered in advertising and commercials. What types of misleading statements have they discovered?

- Make a class "Honest People We Admire" scrapbook. Ask students to work in pairs to research and write a one-page summary of an honest person they admire in the field of sports, politics, science, entertainment, education, the arts, or any field. Have them draw a picture of the person they selected to accompany their report. Bind all of the reports in a class scrapbook to be shared by parents during open house and back-to-school night or by classroom visitors.

- Have a class discussion about organizations such as the Food and Drug Administration (FDA) and the Federal Communications Commission (FCC) that work to ensure honesty in the business world. Ask your students to explore the work these and other organizations do to promote honesty and to protect the public.

Chapter 2
Respect

**regard for and appreciation of worth;
honor and esteem**

A Letter to Parents

Dear Parents,

This month our class will be learning about the value of **respect** through discussions, role-playing, creative writing, and art. We will be learning about showing respect for other people, for respecting differences, and for respecting privacy. We will also learn what it means to show respect for our personal possessions, for property, and for the environment. Not only will we learn about showing respect at home, at school, and out in social situations, we'll also learn about ways people of different cultures and countries show respect.

Whenever possible, take time to talk to your child about respect. Begin by talking about self-respect and what it means. Ask your child to talk about people he or she respects and what qualities these people possess. Help your son or daughter set personal "self-respect" goals to strive for. Discuss the ways in which you were brought up to show respect for your teachers, your parents, and older people. Contrast and compare how times and ways of showing respect have changed. Talk about the expectations you have for your child regarding respecting other people.

Here are other ways you can reinforce the value of respect with your child:

- While watching television together as a family, look for examples of respect (or lack of respect) in the shows you view. Notice how people relate and show respect for one another. Use these incidents as topics for family discussions at dinner time.

- Give your child hypothetical situations concerning respect to see how he or she would handle each situation.

- Read books that deal with the value of respect. Ask your librarian for suggested titles.

Thank you for being our partner in helping to teach your child the value of **respect**. Please feel free to visit our class and see what we're doing to learn more about respect, not only for ourselves but for other people.

Sincerely,

What Is Respect?

In your own words, describe what the word *respect* means.

_____

_____

_____

_____

Find the word *respect* in a dictionary and write its definition below.

_____

_____

_____

_____

Describe a time when you were especially respectful to someone.

_____

_____

_____

_____

Describe a time someone treated you with respect.

_____

_____

_____

_____

How Do You Show Respect?

You are showing respect when you . . .

- talk politely to others
- listen when others are talking and do not interrupt
- get to places on time and don't keep friends or family waiting
- take care of your clothes, books, games, and other possessions
- obey the rules your mom or dad have set at home
- offer your seat on a bus or train to an older person
- treat everyone fairly and kindly
- greet adults you meet for the first time with a firm handshake
- look people straight in the eyes when you talk to them
- show concern for other people
- care for your environment by recycling
- follow classroom rules
- help a teacher substituting in your class for the first time

Discuss how you show respect . . .

- at a school assembly
- at a ball game
- in a synagogue, church, or temple
- in a movie theater
- to people in authority

In what other ways do you show respect?

Setting Goals for Yourself

Set goals for yourself that deal with respect. List goals under each heading below. Think about how you can accomplish each goal.

Respect for Yourself

Respect for Your Family

Respect for Your Teachers

Setting Goals for Yourself
continued

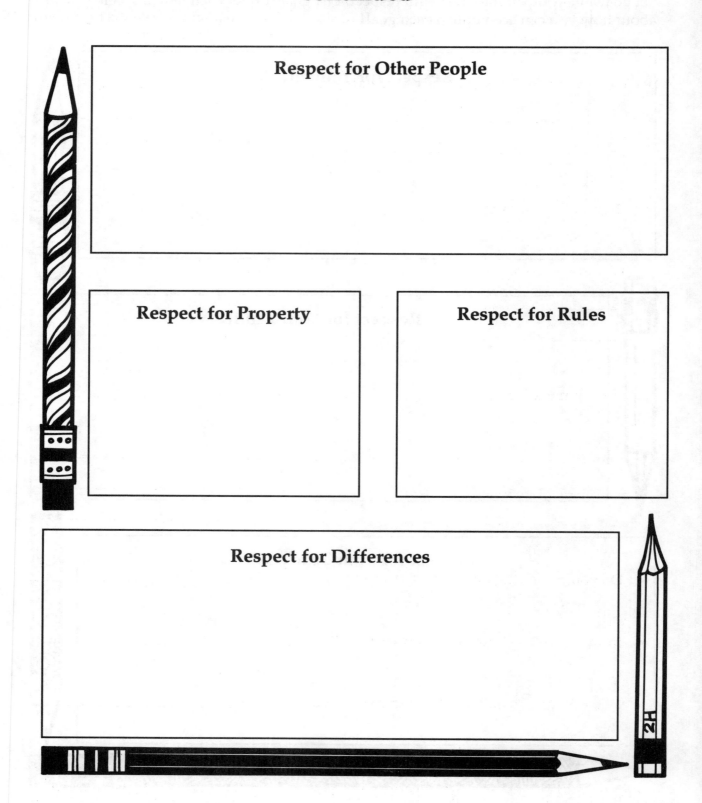

Respect for Other People

Respect for Property

Respect for Rules

Respect for Differences

Respect for Yourself

If you want other people to respect you, it is important for you to respect yourself. You have to feel good about the kind of person you are, the way you treat others, and the things you do each day. Ask yourself these questions and write short answers for each.

- What do you like most about yourself? _____

  _____

  _____

- Do you set goals for yourself? _____

- Would you pick yourself for a friend? Why or why not? _____

  _____

  _____

- Do you make time to spend a few minutes by yourself each day? _____

- How do you try to improve yourself? _____

  _____

  _____

- Do you put forth your best effort at school? _____

- In what ways are you a good friend to others? _____

- What do you consider to be your two best qualities? _____

  _____

  _____

Respect for Yourself
continued

- How do you treat other members of your family? _____

  _____

- Do you help around the house and meet your responsibilities? _____

- How do you help other people at school, at home, or in your community? _____

  _____

  _____

- Describe a time you worked hard to earn money. _____

  _____

  _____

- Are you happy with yourself most of the time? _____

- What are you most proud of in your life? _____

  _____

- What could you do to become a better person? _____

  _____

  _____

  _____

Teaching Values—Reaching Kids
© The Learning Works, Inc.

People You Respect

When you respect people, you admire them and look up to them as role models. You like the way they act towards other people and admire the things they have done with their lives. For each of the categories below, choose a person you respect. Tell who the person is and, on the lines inside each box, describe one special thing you respect about him or her.

a family member

Name _____

_____

_____

_____

_____

_____

someone in your community

Name _____

_____

_____

_____

_____

_____

a friend

Name _____

_____

_____

_____

_____

_____

someone famous
(an author, athlete, politician, scientist, educator, etc.)

Name _____

_____

_____

_____

_____

Showing Respect for People

Pick six of the people below. On a separate piece of paper, write examples of ways you could show respect for the people you selected.

a parent	a brother or sister	a relative	a best friend
a classmate	a teacher	a senior citizen	a coach
a neighbor	a salesperson	your mom's or dad's boss	a police officer
a person with a disability	a waiter or waitress	a person you don't care for	someone you meet for the first time

Role-Playing Respect

Think about what you would do in each of the following situations. Then role-play the situation with several of your classmates. Show the rest of your class how you would show respect for other people and successfully resolve each problem.

You and your mom are riding on the bus. An elderly woman boards the bus carrying a bag of groceries. She looks for an empty seat, but there is none to be found. She stands next to you and holds onto the back of your seat as the bus takes off.

Your class gets rowdy and the teacher tries to get everyone to settle down. The kids are so worked up that no one is listening to your teacher.

Your soccer coach is a member of a minority. You overhear members of an opposing team making unkind remarks about your coach and her race.

A salesperson always treats you with little respect. He ignores you or helps other customers first even though you were there before they were. You think he treats you rudely because you are young.

Respect for Differences

Think of the many ways people are different. For example they might have different ages, heights, weights, skin colors, hair colors, religions, food preferences, birthplaces, or athletic abilities.

Think about other ways people are different. How many differences can you list?

_____   _____

_____   _____

_____   _____

_____   _____

Have people ever treated you badly just because you were different? If so, how did this make you feel? Explain what happened.

_____

_____

_____

_____

Have you ever treated anyone badly just because he or she was different from you in some way? If so, how do you think the person felt? Explain what happened.

_____

_____

_____

_____

Why is it important to respect people who are different from you?

_____

_____

_____

Role-Playing Respect for Differences

Think about what you would do in each of the following situations, then role-play each situation with several of your classmates. Show the rest of your class how you would show respect for differences and successfully resolve each problem.

In the school cafeteria, some of your classmates are making fun of a student who is extremely overweight. They are laughing loudly. The student they are talking about hears them and walks out of the room.

A classmate invites you to a holiday dinner at his house that will include ethnic foods. You don't like to eat food you haven't tried before, but you want to be with your friend and his family for the holiday dinner.

A girl in your class is a very slow learner. She attends special classes during part of the day and is in your class for the remainder of the day. All of the kids ignore her and exclude her from their activities.

You have a friend at school who uses a wheelchair. A group of kids from another class are always making fun of your friend during recess and at lunchtime. You know your friend's feelings are hurt by the constant teasing.

Respect for Privacy

What are your favorite things to do when you have time by yourself? (Check all that apply.)

- [ ] read a book
- [ ] listen to music
- [ ] play with a pet
- [ ] play an instrument

- [ ] watch television
- [ ] use a computer
- [ ] practice a sport
- [ ] other (describe) _____

Where do you go when you want to be by yourself?

_____

_____

_____

Write about a time you were not in the mood to be with other people and just wanted to be by yourself. Did the people around you respect your need for privacy?

_____

_____

_____

_____

Describe a time you failed to respect a family member's need for privacy.

_____

_____

_____

Write about a time you respected a friend's or family member's need for privacy.

_____

_____

_____

Role-Playing Respect for Privacy

Think about what you would do in each of the following situations. Then role-play the situation with several of your classmates. Show the rest of your class how you would show respect for privacy and successfully resolve each problem.

Your parents have recently told you that they are getting a divorce. A classmate wants to know all the details about why your mom and dad are splitting up.

Your best friend has been very sad for the last week. You ask him what's wrong, but he replies, "Just leave me alone!"

Your younger sister is always coming into your room when you are at school or out with friends. She likes to play on your computer. You've asked her many times to stay out of your room.

While cleaning one day, you come across your brother's special notebook. Even though you know the contents are private, you are curious to read what your brother has written.

Respect on the Telephone

Here is a checklist of things to remember when using the telephone.

☐ Ask the person you are calling if it is a good time to talk.

☐ Don't call friends or family during the hours around dinner time.

☐ Keep background noise down when someone is on the phone.

☐ Limit the amount of time you talk on the phone as a courtesy to other family members.

☐ Take accurate phone messages for family members when they are not at home.

☐ Don't interrupt. Wait until the other person on the phone is finished talking before you begin to speak.

☐ If you make a telephone call to request information, don't forget to use the words "please" and "thank you."

54

Design a Stamp

Pretend you have been chosen to design a postage stamp in honor of National Respect Week. Design a stamp that shows ways people can show respect for themselves, for differences among people, for property and personal belongings, or for the environment. Plan your design on scratch paper, and draw your final version on the stamp below. Color your stamp with felt-tipped markers, crayons, or colored pencils.

What Is Respect for Property?

Pick six of the items below. Describe how you show respect
for each of the items you selected.

- your bedroom
- furniture in your house
- your clothes
- the family television or stereo
- items of special value in your home
- your bicycle
- library books and books you own
- computers
- CDs and cassettes
- your family's car
- something you borrow from a friend
- sports equipment
- your school classroom
- your desk at school
- the school grounds
- your neighbor's house and property
- public buildings or parks

On a separate piece of paper, select five other things
not listed above and describe how you would show respect for each.

56

What Would You Do?

Describe what you would do if you saw someone . . .

painting graffiti
on a public building

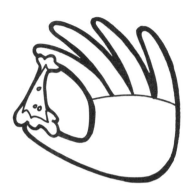

sticking gum underneath
a school desk

tearing a page out of
a library book

picking flowers from
a neighbor's garden
without permission

vandalizing your school

littering a public park,
beach, or campground

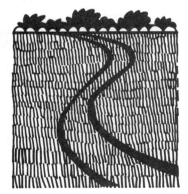

riding a bike on
a neighbor's lawn

stopping up a sink
with paper towels in the
restroom at school

taking something from
someone else's desk

Respect for Rules

What are rules? _____

_____

_____

Why are rules necessary? _____

_____

_____

Why do some people disobey rules? _____

_____

_____

What are some consequences when rules are broken? _____

_____

_____

On a separate piece of paper, write two rules that might be needed for each category:

- at home
- at school
- in a restaurant
- in an auditorium
- while playing a sport
- while riding your bicycle
- in your community

For each item you listed above, discuss with your classmates why the rule is important, how it protects you, how each rule could be enforced, and the consequences of breaking the rule.

Teaching Values—Reaching Kids
© The Learning Works, Inc.

Respect for Rules

Think about a time you disobeyed an important rule. Then, on a separate piece of paper, answer the following questions as honestly as possible. You will not have to share this information with anyone else. This exercise is for your own reflection and growth.

- What were you doing at the time you broke the rule?

- What made you break the rule?

- Were you influenced by anyone else?

- Did you act alone or were others involved?

- Did you get caught? If so, by whom?

- Did you accept the blame for breaking the rule or did you make an excuse?

- How did you feel about what you did?

- What were the consequences of your breaking the rule? Were you punished? If so, what was your punishment?

- Did you feel the punishment was fair? Why or why not?

- What was the importance of the rule?

- Did you ever break the rule again?

- What did you learn from this experience?

Respect for the Environment

You are showing respect for the environment when you pick up a discarded paper cup on a public beach, when you walk around a flower bed rather than trample through it, or when you leave frogs and lizards free to grow up in the wild where they belong.

List examples of how people can show respect for the environment.

_____

_____

_____

_____

Describe a time that you respected the environment. What did you do? How did it make you feel?

_____

_____

_____

_____

Write about a time you saw or read about someone who destroyed the environment instead of respecting it. How did you feel?

_____

_____

_____

_____

Teaching Values—Reaching Kids
© The Learning Works, Inc.

Write a Poem

Write a cinquain poem using **respect** as the main theme. A cinquain poem has five lines and follows this specific structure:

line 1 — one word of two syllables (may be the title)
line 2 — four syllables (describing the subject or title)
line 3 — six syllables (showing action)
line 4 — eight syllables (expressing a feeling or observation about the subject)
line 5 — two syllables (describing the subject)

> **Example:**
>
> Respect
> Kind to people
> Listening and sharing
> Treating others with special care
> And love.

On Your Own

Write a cinquain poem on the lines provided.

_____

_____

_____

_____

_____

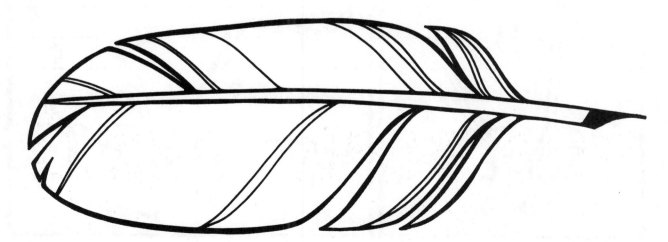

Respect Around the World

Customs differ from culture to culture. For example, in some countries, it is a sign of respect for a woman to walk behind her husband. Pick a country from each continent below. Do research to find unique ways the people of this country show respect. Write a short paragraph about each country on a separate piece of paper. Name the countries you selected and locate them on a map. Share your findings with your classmates.

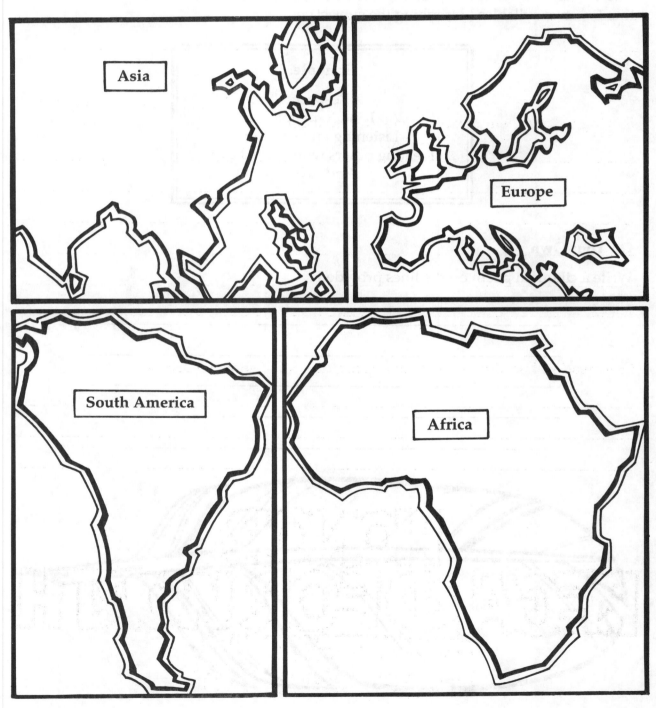

Summing Up Respect

Complete each statement or question.

Something new I learned about respect is _____

_____

_____

_____

Did you reach the "respect" goals you set for yourself? Give examples of how you are moving toward them or have accomplished them.

_____

_____

_____

_____

_____

_____

One area I still need to work on to improve the way I show respect is

_____

_____

_____

Quotes on Respect

- Make the most of yourself, for that is all there is of you.
  Ralph Waldo Emerson

- Without feelings of respect, what is there to distinguish men from beasts?
  Confucius

- If you have some respect for people as they are, you can be more effective in helping them to become better than they are.
  John W. Gardner

- We can always make ourselves liked provided we act likable, but we cannot always make ourselves esteemed, no matter what our merits are.
  Nicolas Malebranche

- I must respect the opinions of others even if I disagree with them.
  Herbert Henry Lehman

- I can live for two months on a good compliment.
  Mark Twain

Student Follow-Up Activities
Respect

- Read your local newspaper, and look for articles that describe times when people didn't respect the rights or property of others. In your own words, tell how the problem could have been avoided.

- Design a mural with your classmates that reflects the theme of respect.

- Write a short skit to perform for younger kids that teaches young children how to respect each other, respect differences, or respect property.

- Show your respect for the elderly by planning a special event at a senior citizens' or retirement home in your community. Your special event could be a visit to cheer up someone's day or a delivery of home-baked cookies. If you plan a visit, be sure to call first and arrange a time that's best for both you and the senior citizens. Check to make sure your intended project will be welcomed. Find out how many people there are so you can plan accordingly. Be sure that your project doesn't conflict with or duplicate other projects the facility has planned.

- Work as a class for a park, trail, or beach clean-up day to show your respect for nature. Be sure to get permission from the owner or manager of the property to make certain that your project doesn't conflict with other plans or projects already scheduled.

- Volunteer to help out at the Special Olympics in your community as a way of showing your respect for people with special needs.

Student Follow-Up Activities
Respect

- Plan a multicultural snack day when your classmates bring a snack to school that represents their cultural heritage. Let everyone taste the various foods so they can learn to appreciate and respect food from different cultures and backgrounds. Make a multicultural recipe book describing how to make each snack.

- Plan a poster contest. Create original messages and pictures to teach others about respect. Display your winning posters in the cafeteria or school office.

- Create a "Respect Week" for your class. Have everyone try to do at least three things each day to show respect for another student, for an adult, for a family member, for nature, or for school or personal property. As a class, make a list of all the things you do.

- For a period of one week, notice how respect and disrespect is portrayed in the television shows you watch. Write a summary of your findings and share it with your class.

- Do research to learn more about respect for the flag. Find out when and how to display the flag on special occasions, how to fold it, and how it is used in ceremonies. Share your findings with your classmates.

Teacher Follow-Up Activities
Respect

- Discuss the proper methods of introducing people. Ask your students to role-play a variety of introductions, such as a parent to a teacher at a back-to-school night or a student to a person with a title such as doctor, professor, or rabbi. Ask your students to brainstorm other social situations where introductions are necessary so they learn the proper skills and ways of showing respect.

- Create a "respect" bulletin board in your classroom. Ask each student to draw a picture of what respect means to them. Their theme could be respect for other people, for animals, for property, or for the environment. Display their completed pictures on your bulletin board for everyone to share. Take time to have each student discuss the meaning of his or her picture.

- Teach your students respect for holidays of various cultures. Divide your class into teams of five or six students. Ask each team to select a different culture, research an important holiday of that culture, and prepare an oral presentation with visual aids to share with the class. To make sure that cultures of Asia, Africa, Europe, and South America are all represented, you might have each team draw the name of a continent for their research. By learning more about the holidays of other cultures, students will gain a deeper understanding of and respect for cultures different from their own.

Chapter 3
Cooperation

**common effort; the act of working
with others for mutual benefit**

A Letter to Parents

Dear Parents,

This month our class will be learning about the value of **cooperation** through discussions, role-playing, creative writing, and art. We will be learning ways to share with our peers and work as a team to accomplish tasks in a more effective and productive manner.

Please take time to talk to your child about ways he or she can cooperate as a family member at home. Talk about each person's role in the family, the responsibilities each has to the successful running of the family as a unit, and how more can be accomplished by working as a team. Also provide practical examples of ways you cooperate with others on your job each day. Discuss how you cooperate with your friends on a daily basis and the outcomes of this team approach.

Provide positive reinforcement by praising your child when he or she works cooperatively at home, at school, or in social situations with peers.

Here are other ways you can reinforce the value of cooperation with your child:

- Give siblings tasks to do as a team such as setting the table, washing the family car, or preparing a meal. Point out how jobs get done quicker and more efficiently when people work together and each person does his or her share.

- Make up hypothetical situations for your child that involve working cooperatively with others, for example, working on a group project at school or planning a surprise birthday party for a friend. Discuss ways of addressing the problems that arise when an individual doesn't do his or her share of the work.

Thank you for working with us to help teach your child about **cooperation**. Please feel free to visit our class and see what we're doing to learn more about the value of cooperation.

Sincerely,

What is Cooperation?

In your own words, describe what *cooperation* means.

_____

_____

_____

_____

Find the word *cooperation* in the dictionary and write its definition below.

_____

_____

_____

_____

Describe a time you worked cooperatively with other family members to accomplish a task at home.

_____

_____

_____

_____

Describe a time you worked cooperatively with your classmates to accomplish a task at school.

_____

_____

_____

_____

What Are Examples of Cooperation?

You are showing cooperation when you . . .

- work in a small study group at school to review for an upcoming test

- allow each person in a group have a say so his or her opinion can be heard

- try to use everyone's ideas while working in a committee or group

- do your fair share of the work when participating on a team school report

- work with a partner on a science fair project for school

- pitch in at home doing chores so everything runs smoothly

- paint part of a classroom mural with your peers

- play soccer, basketball, or any sport where you are part of a team working towards a common goal

- participate on a student council committee to solve a problem or complete a project

- plan a party with your peers for a classmate

- work with your friends to help clean up a beach or neighborhood park

What are some other ways you show cooperation at home, at school, or with your friends? List as many examples of cooperation as you can.

Setting Goals for Yourself

Set goals for yourself that deal with cooperation. List goals under each heading below. Think about how you can accomplish each goal.

Cooperating with your parents

Cooperating with your brothers and sisters

Cooperating with your friends

Cooperating with your teacher(s)

What is Compromise?

In your own words, describe what *compromise* means?

_____

_____

_____

Find the word *compromise* in the dictionary and write its definition below.

_____

_____

_____

Why is compromise important when you work cooperatively in a group?

_____

_____

_____

Think about times you've had a different viewpoint from someone else during one of these situations:

- during a family discussion
- while working with your classmates on a project at school
- on the school playground
- when playing a team sport
- while out with your friends
- while on a trip or vacation

Pick one situation and on a separate piece of paper describe how you compromised to resolve the issue. Describe the compromise you reached. Tell what you and the other person or people gave up to reach this compromise and work the problem out. How did you feel about the outcome?

Cooperation at School

What are some of the benefits of working cooperatively on school projects?

_____

_____

_____

How does working cooperatively help you get to know your classmates better?

_____

_____

_____

Briefly tell how working cooperatively helps you learn each skill listed below—skills you'll use throughout your life.

- solving conflicts:

- compromising:

- listening carefully to others:

- communicating your ideas to other people:

- understanding viewpoints that differ from yours:

- working together to achieve a common goal:

Word Search Puzzle

What words do you think of when you think of the word *cooperation*? Sharing? Listening? Compromising? Select twelve words and write them on the lines below.

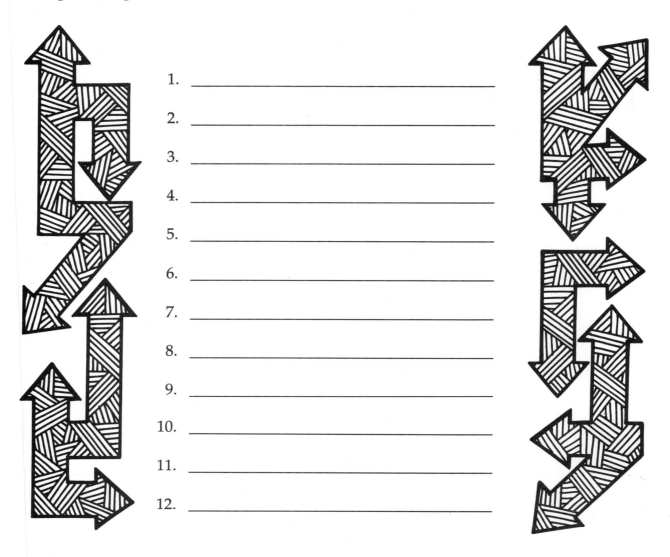

1. _____
2. _____
3. _____
4. _____
5. _____
6. _____
7. _____
8. _____
9. _____
10. _____
11. _____
12. _____

Now make a word search puzzle using the words you listed above. Write your twelve words going up, down, backwards, forward, and diagonally in the grid on page 77. On the lines provided, make a list of the words hidden in your puzzle.

76

Word Search Puzzle

Use the words you listed on page 76 to create a word search puzzle. You can write the words going up, down, forwards, backwards, and diagonally in the puzzle. Fill in all the blank squares with different letters of the alphabet, one per box. Give your puzzle to a classmate to solve.

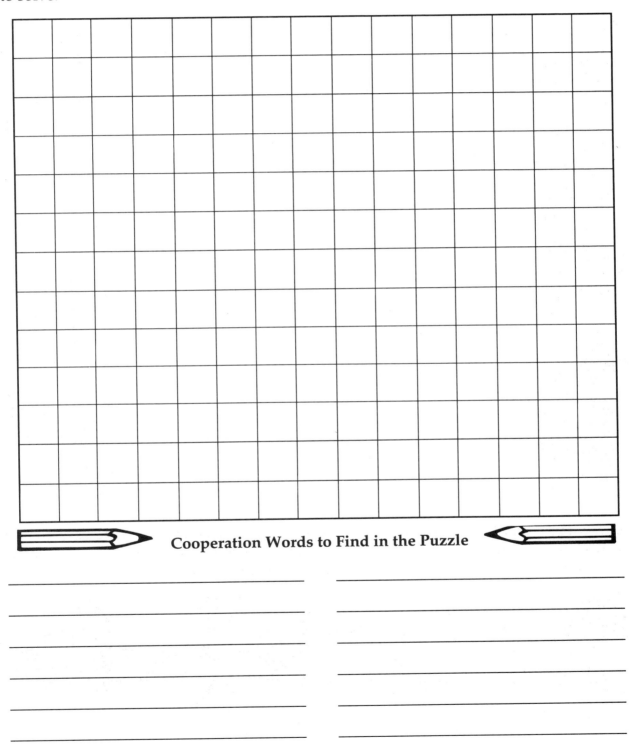

Cooperation Words to Find in the Puzzle

Before You Begin

When working cooperatively on a school project, it is helpful to create a planning sheet to assist you in organizing your ideas and setting goals for your group.

On a separate sheet of paper create a planning sheet for your next group project. Here are some topics you might want to include:

- Title and explanation of our project

- Date our project is due

- Our goals

- How we plan to reach the goals we've set

- Assigned tasks for each member of our group

- Times and places we'll meet to work on our project

- How we plan to evaluate our results

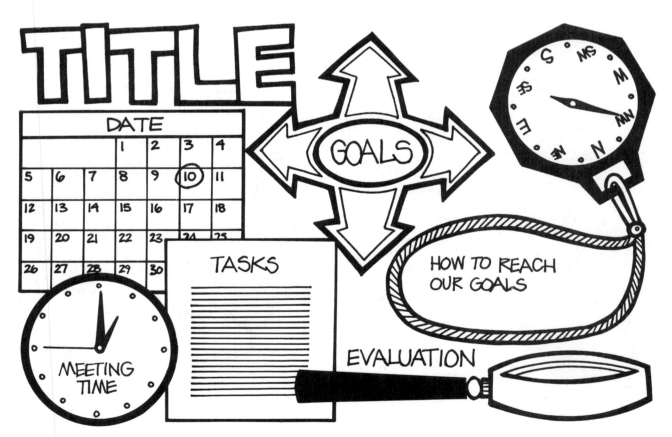

Guidelines for Cooperative Learning

Here are some guidelines you can follow to help things run smoother and to promote cooperation among your peers when working on group projects at school. As a class, add your own cooperative learning guidelines to this list. Then make a poster of these guidelines to display in your classroom and use as a reminder when working on group projects.

1. Be a good listener when other members of your group are speaking.

2. Distribute the work evenly among team members. Each person should have one or more jobs to do.

3. Encourage each member of the group to contribute his or her ideas. Take time to compliment other members of your team for their contributions.

4. Try to incorporate each person's ideas—not just those of a few members.

5. Treat each member of the group with respect. Be patient and help those who need more guidance. Avoid bossing team members around or making fun of ideas they contribute.

6. Don't get upset and angry if someone on your team offers constructive criticism of your ideas. Be open and receptive to new ideas.

7. If your group can't reach a decision, try to compromise to resolve your differences. Take time to try to see the other person's point of view.

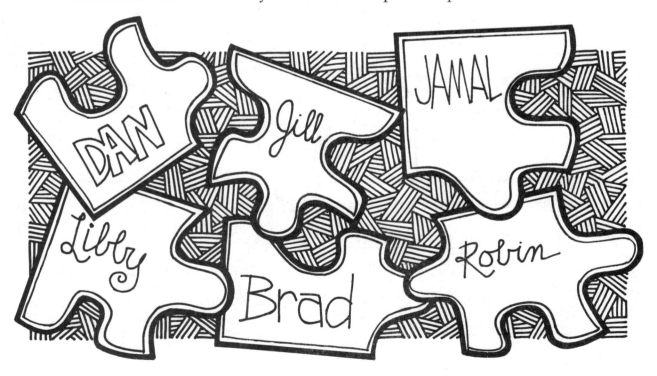

Cooperation Cube

Work together with three or four classmates to make a "cooperation cube." For this project, your team will pick a theme and decorate a box with drawings or magazine pictures to display in your class.

What You Need

- cardboard box
- scissors
- glue
- old magazines for pictures or slogans
- felt-tipped markers
- colored paper
- tape

What You Do

1. As a group, choose a theme for your cube. Decide who will bring each of the things you will need.
2. Cover the box using colored paper and tape.
3. Decorate the four sides and the top of your cube with pictures and slogans from old magazines to tie in with the theme you selected as a group. (If you prefer, draw your own sketches and words.)
4. Display your cooperation cube in class.

Evaluation

- How did your group decide on a theme? _____

  _____

- Did everyone in the group get a chance to present his or her ideas? _____

- Did everyone cooperate and do his or her share of the work? _____

- What did you learn from this experience? _____

  _____

- Did you have a positive experience? _____

- In what ways was it difficult to work together? _____

  _____

- What would you do differently next time? _____

  _____

Cooperation Comics

In the spaces below, create a cartoon story about cooperation. Write your title in the first box. In your cartoon, show how your characters resolve an issue having to do with getting along and pitching in. Use bubbles to show the dialogue your characters speak.

Cooperative Learning Project Ideas

Here are suggestions for projects you can work on cooperatively with your classmates. Each of these projects offers various jobs that people in your group can do according to their strengths and special interests. Some of these projects require research, writing, art, construction, recording, and other skills, thus giving each member of your group a chance to participate in a constructive way.

- **Build a City**
  Start by brainstorming all the things that make up a city: residential areas, schools, hospitals, airports, restaurants, department stores, libraries, police stations, fire stations, etc. Then build your own model city using boxes, cartons, cans, and other recycled materials to represent the buildings you planned. Be sure to include different modes of transportation, as well as parks, lakes, rivers, etc.

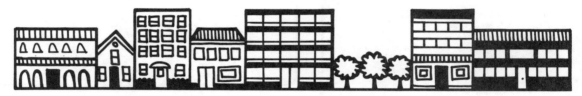

- **Invent a Holiday**
  As a group, decide what you want to celebrate. Then choose a date for your new holiday and describe how your holiday is celebrated. Your group might write a theme song for your holiday, describe games or other activities that people can participate in, or make up some recipes for special holiday foods.

- **Design a Game**
  Design a new board game to help other students review for an academic topic such as spelling, math, history, science, or reading. For example, a math-based game might emphasize addition, subtraction, multiplication, or division skills. Your game should include a game board, playing tokens, question cards, "chance" cards, a spinner or dice, and rules and directions for play. As a group, decide on a theme for your game and the main object of your game: to be the first to cross a finish line, to be the person who gets the most points, etc. Decorate a box so that all the parts of the game can be kept in one place.

Evaluating a Group Project

To help you evaluate your contributions to a group project at school, here are some questions to ask yourself:

- How did you feel about your contributions to the group?

- What do you feel were your strengths?

- How could you improve next time?

- What were the advantages of working with others on the project?

- What did you learn about working cooperatively with others instead of working by yourself?

- In what ways did you make compromises as you worked?

- In what ways did working with others change your thinking?

Cooperation at Home

There are many tasks involved in keeping a home running smoothly. Here are just a few jobs that have to be done on a regular basis.

shop for groceries	dust and vacuum	collect recyclables	feed pets
prepare meals	make beds	clean bathrooms	walk the dog
wash dishes or load dishwasher	wash windows	mow the lawn	wash the car
do laundry	take out garbage	water plants	pay bills

How many other tasks can you list?

_____   _____

_____   _____

_____   _____

Cooperation at Home
(continued)

Look at chart and the tasks listed on page 84 and answer the following questions.

1. In your family, who is mainly responsible for each of the tasks listed? Using the following code, write the answers in each box and beside the additional tasks you listed on page 84.

   D — dad

   M — mom

   Me — if you are responsible for the task

   S — sister

   B — brother

2. In what ways do you help your family?

   _____

   _____

3. Do you believe you do your fair share around the house? Do you feel that too much or too little is asked of you?

   _____

   _____

   _____

4. Do you think the work is evenly and fairly divided among all the members of your household capable of performing these tasks? If not, what would you change?

   _____

   _____

   _____

What If's?

Think about each of the following situations and discuss with your classmates how cooperation would play a major role.

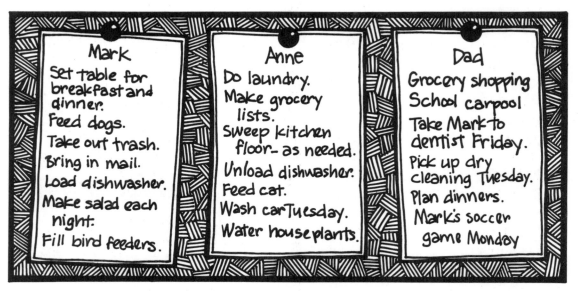

The doctor has told your mother that she must stay in bed for at least a week to help her recover from a recent illness. How will this affect your family? Describe what other family members can do to cooperate and help keep things running smoothly at home until she's feeling better.

Your grandfather is coming from out of town to stay with your family for two weeks. He is going to share your room with you during his visit. Discuss things you can do to make his visit special. What can each member of your family do to help him enjoy his time with you?

What If's?
(continued)

Your next-door neighbors had a serious fire in their home. The family and their pets escaped, but extensive damage was done to their home. The kitchen, living room, and one of the bedrooms were destroyed in the fire. You and your family decide to get together with some of the other neighbors and see how everyone can chip in to help this family in need. What jobs need to be done? What supplies, furniture, or services could be provided? How many ways can you think of that people could help this family? How can other people in the neighborhood—both adults and kids—work together?

As part of a class unit on history, you are asked to do a group project with four other students. Your project will include researching, writing, and map-making, as well as making timelines, models, and oral presentations. You will all share the work and all share the same grade on the completed project. What steps can you take to make sure that each person does his or her share? What are the ways your group can work cooperatively to complete the assignment?

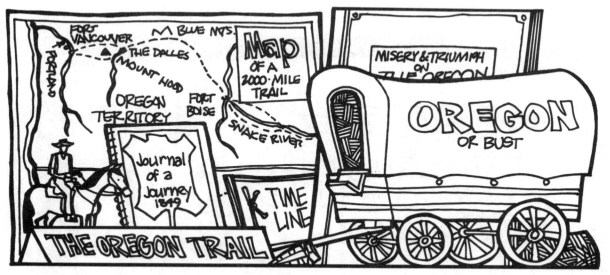

Role-Playing Compromise

Compromise goes hand in hand with working and playing cooperatively with others. No one can get their way all the time. Part of learning how to get along with others is learning how to give in to resolve differences and reach common goals. Think about what you would do in each of the following situations. Then role-play the situation with several of your classmates. Show the rest of your class ways you could compromise to successfully resolve each problem.

You are working on a state report with three other classmates. Your group has to present information on the state's major cities, physical features, weather, industries, historical landmarks, etc. Everyone in your group is arguing about who is going to be responsible for all of the information needed for the final report.

You and a friend have made arrangements to go to the movie on the weekend. Each of you wants to see a different movie.

Role-Playing Compromise
(continued)

You've been invited to go on a ski trip with a friend's family. You've never been skiing before but you would like to try the sport. Your parents refuse to let you go because they feel it is too dangerous.

Your mom insists that you go with her to visit your grandmother in a nearby nursing home every weekend. Your grandmother is not in good health, and your mom feels it's important for you to spend time with her each week. You want to spend the weekends with your friends or just relaxing.

Cooperation on the Job

In almost every job you can think of, people have to work, relate, and share ideas with other people.

Select four of the occupations below (or list occupations of your own choice). For each occupation you choose, describe ways people might work cooperatively with others on the job. Think about situations that might arise for each occupation where more could be accomplished by sharing ideas and tasks rather than by working alone.

architect
athlete
attorney
chef
chorus singer
coach
construction worker
dentist
doctor
farmer
fire fighter
gardener
lawyer
librarian
mayor
mechanic
nurse
pilot
plumber
police officer
salesperson
teacher
waiter/waitress

The Spirit of Cooperation

There are many ways people within a community can work cooperatively to improve their neighborhoods or help other people. They can form a group to clean up a park, work together to repair the home of a family in need, or organize a food drive to feed the less fortunate.

In each box below, illustrate a way people can work cooperatively to help others. Write a brief description below each box.

Writing About Cooperation

During natural disasters, people often come together to help their neighbors and friends. Newspaper articles tell about people who provide coffee and sandwiches for rescue workers, who help neighbors rebuild homes that have burned to the ground during a fire, or who donate clothes and furniture to friends who have lost all of their belongings after a hurricane.

Select one of the following projects to write about:

1. Write a short story about a community that pulls together to help each other out after one of the following natural disasters:

   - an earthquake

   - a flood

   - a wildfire

   - a hurricane

   - a tornado

   - a mudslide

2. Write a poem about people working to help each other after a natural disaster.

3. Pretend you are a newspaper reporter covering a story about a group of people who do something special for a person or family in need. Be sure to answer the following questions in your article: Who? What? Where? Why? and When?

4. Pretend you are a writer for a radio show. Write copy for a two-minute spot about cooperation. Your story could be about people helping their neighbors during a disaster or a group of people working together to improve their community.

Summing Up Cooperation

Complete each statement or question.

Something new I learned about cooperation is _____

_____

_____

_____

Did you reach the "cooperation" goals you set for yourself? Give examples of ways you cooperated or compromised to resolve differences.

_____

_____

_____

_____

_____

When it comes to cooperation, one area I still need to improve in is _____

_____

_____

_____

When it comes to cooperation, one area I excel in is _____

_____

_____

_____

TEAM SPIRIT PARTNERSHIP COORDINATION

Quotes on Cooperation

- Better bend than break.
  Scottish proverb

- Clapping with the right hand only will not produce a noise.
  Malay proverb

- We must learn to live together as brothers or perish together as fools.
  Martin Luther King

- On this shrunken globe, men can no longer live as strangers.
  Adlai E. Stevenson

- When spider webs unite, they can tie up a lion.
  Ethiopian proverb

- A single arrow is easily broken, but not ten in a bundle.
  Japanese proverb

When spider webs unite, they can tie up a lion.

Ethiopian proverb

Student Follow-Up Activities
Cooperation

- Get together with your classmates and form teams of five to six students. Each team then writes a song on cooperation to present to the class. Your team can write an original song or can put words to a popular tune that everyone knows how to sing such as "America, the Beautiful" or "Yankee Doodle Dandy." The lyrics, or words to your song, should convey an important message about the value of cooperation. Have fun by adding homemade musical instruments or props when you perform for your audience. You can even make "sing-along" song sheets so your classmates can sing along with your group.

- Work cooperatively with your classmates to plan a "Beautify Our School Week." Start by getting permission from your teacher and principal. Take a tour around your school to find areas that need beautifying. You might discover an area that could use some plants to perk it up or a place that is overgrown with weeds and needs clearing. Plan what action needs to be taken, who will do each task, and how you will accomplish your goals. If this project is a success, you might want to try it again later in the school year and involve other classes at your school. This kind of team project is a great way to foster school spirit and to teach everyone about the value of cooperating and working together for a common goal.

- Think about a career you might like to pursue as an adult. In what ways would you work cooperatively with other people on the job? For example, if you decided to become a teacher, you would not only be working and interacting with children, but also with other teachers, the principal, administrators, parents, and classroom aides. Write a short play describing how you resolve a problem involving cooperation while at work in the future.

Student Follow-Up Activities
Cooperation

- There are many examples of countries working together for a common goal. For example, the United States and Russia have teamed up to send satellites into space to obtain information that is of interest to both countries. Do research and find other examples of countries working cooperatively. Discuss the results of your research with your classmates. Then make a classroom bulletin board to share your findings.

- Animals work together to gather food, find or build their homes, and insure their survival. For example, in an ant colony, each ant has a specific job to do. Do research to find out what responsibility each of the following ants has: the queen, the workers, the males. Read to discover how ants work together to protect their nests and defend themselves from their enemies. Have fun finding out how other animals work together. Share your findings with your classmates in an oral presentation. Use visual aids such as drawings, photographs, magazine pictures, or graphs to enhance your presentation.

- Create three original quotations about cooperation. Then pick your favorite quote to illustrate and place on a classroom bulletin board for your classmates to enjoy.

Teacher Follow-Up Activities
Cooperation

- To provide practice in cooperative learning skills and to reinforce geography and map skills, try this activity. Divide your class into teams of five or six students. Give each team a blank outline of the United States. Ask the students to fill in the name of each state as well as the major mountain ranges, rivers, oceans, and lakes. Let members of each group evaluate how their team worked together and answer the following questions:

  - Did everyone have an opportunity to participate?
  - Who took leadership roles?
  - How were differences resolved when team members couldn't agree?
  - Was each team member treated with respect?
  - What were the advantages of doing this activity as a group?
  - What were the disadvantages?
  - What did the students learn about themselves?
  - What did the students learn about their teammates?
  - What would each team do differently next time?

- Tie in the theme of cooperation with the unit your class is currently studying in social studies. For example, if your class is studying the Westward Movement, discuss ways people had to work cooperatively for their survival. Ask your students to consider how people worked together on their jobs, in setting up camp, while on the trail, for defense, and to fulfill other needs during this period.

- Let students work with a partner to complete a math homework assignment. After the assignment is complete, ask them to evaluate why two heads are better than one. Discuss any problems the partners encountered and how they settled differences while working together.

- Ask the students in your class to create a mural for your school office, multipurpose room, or cafeteria. During this activity, the entire class should work cooperatively in the planning, execution, and presentation of the mural.

Chapter 4
Perseverance

**the act or habit of continuing
to strive in spite of difficulties**

A Letter to Parents

Dear Parents,

This month our class will be learning about the value of **perseverance** through discussions, role-playing, creative writing, and art. We will learn about men and women who have overcome various disabilities to achieve greatness in their fields. We will also learn about overcoming hardships such as poverty and prejudice. We'll learn about setting our own short- and long-range goals for both home and school.

Whenever possible, please take time to talk to your child about perseverance. Share your own personal experiences of growing up and working through hard times. Talk about times in your life when you set goals and the outcomes of these goals—both your successes and your failures. Talk to your child about times you failed to stick to a task and the consequences you faced. Share rewarding moments you had in your life and how you felt about yourself.

Provide positive reinforcement for efforts your son or daughter makes toward setting goals and achieving them. If your child fails to reach a goal, talk about ways he or she could approach the situation in the future.

Here are other ways you can reinforce the value of perseverance with your child at home:

- Stress with your child the importance of setting small, realistic goals. Remind him or her that perseverance doesn't come quickly or easily.

- Have an informal family meeting once a week and ask each member of your family to set three goals for the coming week. The goals could pertain to school, work, play, or family life. Write each person's goals down and evaluate them at your next meeting.

- Visit your public library and read books about people who have persevered through difficult times or situations. Use the list of famous men and women on page 103 or ask your librarian for suggestions of other people to read about.

Thank you for working with us in helping to teach your child about the value of **perseverance**. Please feel free to visit our class and see what we're doing to learn more about perseverance.

Sincerely,

What Is Perseverance?

In your own words, describe what the word *perseverance* means.

_____

_____

_____

_____

Find the word *perseverance* in the dictionary and write its definition below.

_____

_____

_____

Describe a time you showed perseverance at home or school.

_____

_____

_____

_____

_____

Describe how you felt after reaching a difficult goal that took a long time to achieve.

_____

_____

_____

_____

_____

What Are Examples of Perseverance?

You are showing perseverance when you . . .

- give up your television time to spend hours and hours studying for the school spelling bee

- try a new sport that's very difficult for you and you don't give up

- have a learning disability and keep studying even though you are feeling discouraged

- come from a home where there is constant fighting and unhappiness but still try your best at whatever you do

- have missed a week of school because of illness but you work a little longer and harder each night to make up the schoolwork you missed

- are near the end of a difficult race and then, just when you think you aren't going to be able to finish, find a burst of energy so you can cross the finish line

- have lost a leg because of cancer and still learn how to ski

- save money and make sacrifices for a long time in order to buy something you really want

- spend afternoons and weekends practicing on your trumpet so you can play well in the school band

- try out for a spot on the team for a second time after you don't make it the first time around

- study and work hard to raise your grade in a certain subject at school

People Who Persevered

Here is a list of some famous people who have worked hard to overcome their disabilities and do something special with their lives.

Ludwig Van Beethoven	musician	deaf
Ray Charles	musician, composer	blind
Thomas Edison	inventor, scientist	learning disability
Albert Einstein	scientist	learning disability
Terry Fox	runner	amputee with cancer
Stephen Hawking	physicist, author	Lou Gehrig's disease
James Earl Jones	actor	stutterer (ages 6-14)
Helen Keller	author, lecturer	deaf and blind
Marlee Matlin	actress	deaf
Itzhak Perlman	concert violinist	paralyzed (from the waist down)
Franklin Delano Roosevelt	32nd president of the United States	polio from polio (at age 39)
Vincent Van Gogh	artist	mentally ill
Woodrow Wilson	27th president of the United States	learning disability
Stevie Wonder	musician	blind

People Who Persevered
(continued)

1. Choose a person from the list on page 103 or select a famous man or woman who you feel has persevered in life and overcome great hardships. Do research to learn more about this person's life. Write a report describing the challenges this person faced and how he or she overcame them to achieve success.

2. Look in newspapers and magazines for articles about people who have done something special with their lives. Cut them out and post these on a classroom bulletin board for classmates to read and to learn about.

3. Write a short story about a person with a disability who becomes a hero. The main character in your story could have a physical disability or a learning disability. Show how he or she displayed perseverance to overcome this disability.

4. Do you know a friend or family member who has shown perseverance? Prepare a list of interesting questions and then interview this person to learn more about his or her life. Share his or her story with your classmates.

What Are Goals?

Many people have overcome their personal weaknesses and turned them into strengths. People with learning disabilities such as Albert Einstein and Winston Churchill have gone on to accomplish great things in their lives and for the benefit of others. These people and others have persevered in spite of weaknesses because they set goals for themselves and never gave up trying to achieve their goals.

On a separate piece of paper, answer each of the following questions:

- What are goals?

- Why do people set goals?

- What are examples of short-range goals someone might set for an hour, a day, or a week?

- What are examples of long-range goals someone might set for a month, a year, or several years down the road?

- Have you ever set goals for yourself?

- If so, did you just think about them or did you write them down?

- Do you think it helps to write your goals down? Why or why not?

- What are some goals you have met?

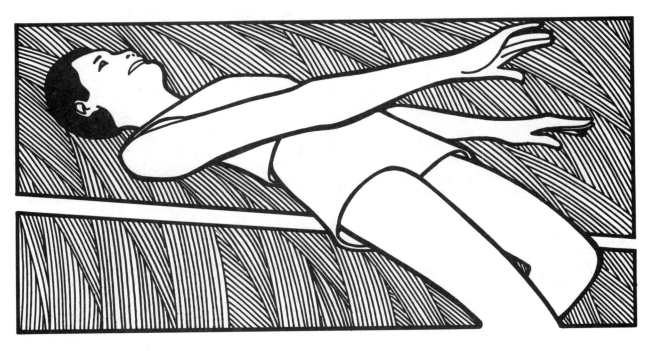

Sticking to Your Goals

Some people stick to a task or goal until it is completed while others give up along the way. Many times there are important and valid reasons for not reaching a goal Have you ever given up a goal for any of the following reasons? (Check all that apply.)

☐ illness or injury

☐ influence of your friends

☐ influence of your family

☐ the task was too hard

☐ the task was too easy

☐ loss of interest

☐ not enough time

☐ the goal was unrealistic

☐ personal problems at school

☐ personal problems at home

☐ not enough money

☐ it became unimportant

☐ other reasons (describe) _____

On a separate piece of paper, write about a time:

• you set a goal for yourself but failed because of one of the reasons you checked above.

• you set a goal for yourself at home or at school and successfully achieved your goal.

In each case, describe what it was you were trying to accomplish, what steps you to took towards achieving it, and why you were or were not successful. Describe how you felt about yourself in each example. Tell what you would do differently the next time. Would you pursue this goal again? Why or why not?

Setting Short-Range Goals for Yourself

Under each heading below, list one short-range goal for yourself. Describe why each goal is important to you. On a separate piece of paper, make a list of small steps you can take to help your reach each goal. Use this as a checklist as you work toward your goals.

AT HOME

Something I can accomplish tomorrow:

Things I can accomplish this week:

AT SCHOOL

Things I can accomplish tomorrow:

Things I can accomplish this week:

OTHER GOALS (WITH MY FRIENDS, AT SPORTS, ETC.)

Things I can accomplish tomorrow:

Things I can accomplish this week:

Setting Long-Range Goals for Yourself

List one important long-range goal for yourself under each heading. Describe why each goal is important to you. On a separate piece of paper, make a list of small steps you can take to help you reach each goal. Use this as a checklist as you work toward your goals.

AT HOME

Things I can accomplish in the next few months:

Things I can accomplish by next year:

AT SCHOOL

Things I can accomplish in the next few months:

Things I can accomplish by next year:

OTHER GOALS (WITH MY FRIENDS, AT SPORTS, ETC.)

Things I can accomplish in the next few months:

Things I can accomplish by next year:

The Meaning of Success

Whether it's studying for an important exam in school, or putting in long, hard hours on a job as an adult, part of perseverance is striving to reach goals you set for yourself and being successful in whatever you do. But what is success? Is it fame, wealth, happiness, self-satisfaction, or excellence?

I think success is _____

_____

One time I felt very successful at school was when I _____

_____

_____

One time I felt very successful at home was when I _____

_____

_____

One time I succeeded in a sport or game was when I _____

_____

_____

In the future, I'd like to succeed in _____

_____

I'd like to be famous for _____

_____

> We are a success:
> . . . When we fill a niche and accomplish a task. When we leave the world better than we found it, whether by an improved idea, a perfect poem, or a rescued soul. We are successful if we never lack appreciation of earth's beauty or fail to express it. If we look for the best in others, and give the best we have.
> —*Robert Louis Stevenson*

Thinking About Goals for the Future

No one can predict the future, but it's fun to think about what your life might be like in the days and years to come. Write short answers for each of the following:

a hobby I'd like to explore _____

a sport, game, or skill I'd like to learn _____

a summer job I'd like to have when I'm older _____

a way I'd like to help other people _____

a state I'd like to visit_____

a country I'd like to visit _____

a career I think I'd enjoy _____

a place I'd like to live_____

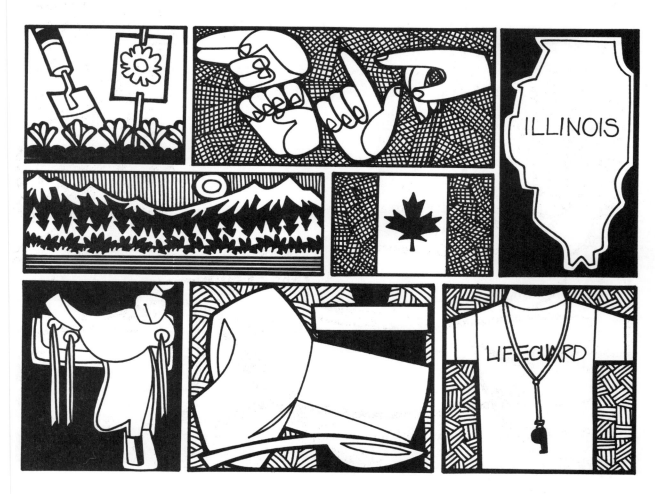

Write a Fable

A *fable* is a fictitious or supernatural story that usually teaches a moral. Often, talking animals are used as the main characters of fables, as in the story of *The Tortoise and the Hare*.

On a separate sheet of paper, write a fable about two animal characters who learn an important lesson about perseverance. Draw illustrations for your fable.

Here are some ideas for animals you could use as the main characters in your fable.

baboon	kangaroo
badger	lion
bear	monkey
beaver	mouse
camel	ostrich
cat	otter
cow	panda
coyote	peacock
deer	possum
dog	raccoon
donkey	rhinoceros
elephant	sheep
fox	skunk
frog	tiger
giraffe	turtle
goat	whale
goose	yak
hyena	zebra

Two Miles to Go

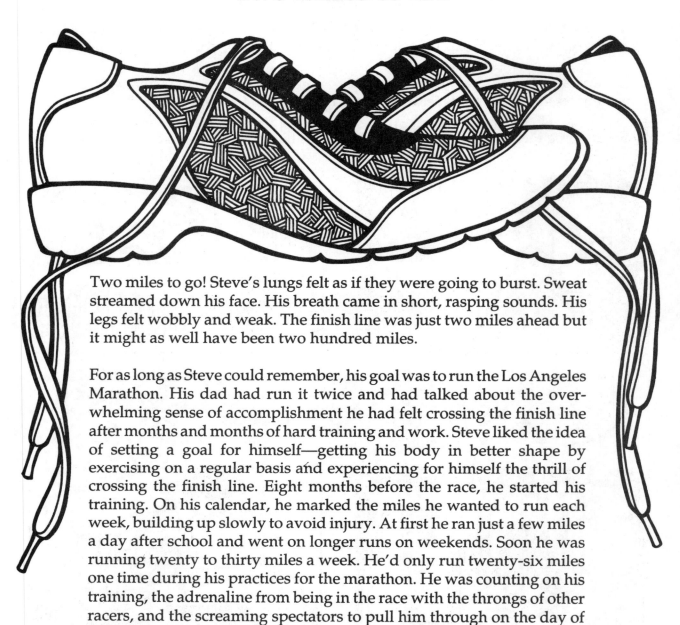

Two miles to go! Steve's lungs felt as if they were going to burst. Sweat streamed down his face. His breath came in short, rasping sounds. His legs felt wobbly and weak. The finish line was just two miles ahead but it might as well have been two hundred miles.

For as long as Steve could remember, his goal was to run the Los Angeles Marathon. His dad had run it twice and had talked about the overwhelming sense of accomplishment he had felt crossing the finish line after months and months of hard training and work. Steve liked the idea of setting a goal for himself—getting his body in better shape by exercising on a regular basis and experiencing for himself the thrill of crossing the finish line. Eight months before the race, he started his training. On his calendar, he marked the miles he wanted to run each week, building up slowly to avoid injury. At first he ran just a few miles a day after school and went on longer runs on weekends. Soon he was running twenty to thirty miles a week. He'd only run twenty-six miles one time during his practices for the marathon. He was counting on his training, the adrenaline from being in the race with the throngs of other racers, and the screaming spectators to pull him through on the day of the race.

Now he was actually running the Los Angeles Marathon—a little over twenty-six miles through the heart of Los Angeles. Crowds of cheering spectators lined both sides of the street. Steve knew his family and several of his friends were waiting at the finish line to cheer him across. But Steve didn't know if he was going to make it. His entire body protested in pain, and to make matters worse, a hill loomed ahead. Suddenly . . .

(Finish the story on a separate piece of paper.)

Role-Playing Perseverance

Think about what you would do in each of the following situations. Then role-play the situation with several of your classmates. Demonstrate to the rest of the class how you would show perseverance while solving each problem.

Lisa has a learning disability. School is very hard for her and the other kids in her class make fun of her. It's gotten to the point where she doesn't want to go to school.

Carol is trying to persuade her mom into letting her continue with gymnastics even though she has been injured numerous times while doing routines.

Jamal has missed a week of school because he caught measles from his younger sister. He's fallen behind in his studies and feels like he will never be able to make up all the work he has missed and catch up with his classmates.

Ruben plays basketball on a youth group team after school. He's not a very good player and doesn't get chosen to play as often as other members on the team. He's become discouraged and wants to quit the team. What are some ways Ruben could become a better player?

The Ups and Downs of Life

Like a rollercoaster, life has its ups and downs. There are times when you're "up" and feel as if you could conquer the world. Other times, you feel "down" or sad for no apparent reason. Part of growing up is learning how to handle the ups and downs that life throws your way.

Sometimes when you're "down," you might feel like you are the only person who has ever felt this way. But in talking about your feelings, you'd be surprised to discover that many other kids have felt exactly the same way or have been confronted with similar problems.

Here's a way to learn how some of your peers have handled problems in their lives and have persevered through difficult times.

As a whole class or in small groups, discuss how you would handle each of these "down" situations. If any of these situations have actually happened to you, describe the steps you took to help you resolve the problem or situation.

- you lose a final game that was very important to you
- you do poorly on a test you studied for
- one of your parents loses their job
- your family pet dies
- your best friend moves away
- you are diagnosed with diabetes
- your family's home and everything in it are destroyed in a fire
- your parents decide to get a divorce
- someone close to you is critically ill or has been hurt in an accident
- your grandparent dies

Describe some other "down" situations and how you would handle them.

114

Perseverance to a Tee

Pretend you have been selected to design a t-shirt to be worn by a Special Olympian or some other person who has shown perseverance. Sketch your design on scratch paper, then draw your final design below. Add a message or slogan. Color your drawing with felt-tipped markers, crayons, or colored pencils.

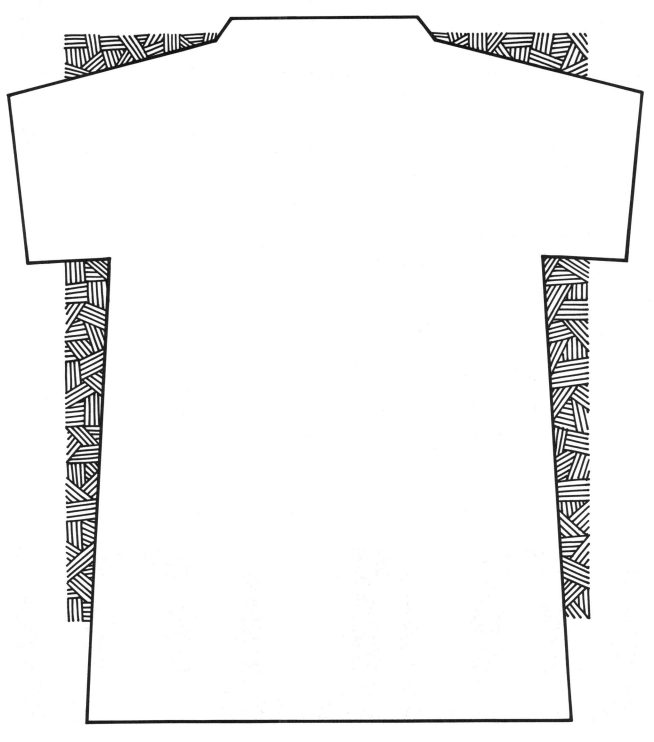

Guest Speakers

Your community is filled with men and women who have persevered in their personal lives or in the business world. Invite some of these people to your class as guest speakers.

Ideas

> **Invite someone who started his or her own business.**
> Suggestions for questions to ask:

- How and when did you get the idea for your business?

- How did you get started?

- What were the most difficult challenges you faced?

- What helped you keep going during difficult times?

- What would you do differently if you had to do it all over again?

- What did you learn from starting your own business?

> **Invite someone with a disability.**
> Suggestions for questions to ask:

- Could you describe your disability so we can learn more about it?

- What special challenges do you face because of your disability?

- How have you learned to overcome your disability?

- What things have helped you the most in dealing with your special challenges?

- In what ways can other people help you?

- What has helped you persevere during hard times?

116

Guest Speakers
(continued)

Invite someone who has accomplished something outstanding or who has won a special award or honor.

Suggestions for questions to ask:

- What award did you win?

- What did you do to win this honor or award?

- Did you set personal goals for yourself prior to winning this award?

- What obstacles did you face in trying to achieve your goals?

- What sacrifices did you make in order to accomplish this?

- How did you overcome these obstacles?

- What helped you persevere?

- What did you learn from this experience?

- What advice would you give young people today?

Invite someone who has come here from another country.

Suggestions for questions to ask:

- What country did you come from?

- Why did you leave there?

- What surprised you most about this country?

- What difficulties have you experienced here?

- What things do you miss most about your native land?

A Poem About Perseverance

A **tanka** is a verse form similar to haiku, except two more lines are added to the poem. The tanka uses the following structure:

Pattern:

line 1—five syllables
line 2—seven syllables
line 3—five syllables
line 4—seven syllables
line 5—seven syllables

Examples:

Sticking to your goals
Nothing standing in your way
Aiming for the top
Makes you feel so good inside
Knowing you have succeeded.

Math test is next week.
Won't wait for the last minute
Start to study now
Review a little each day
I'm going to ace this test!

On a separate sheet of paper, write a tanka poem about perseverance.

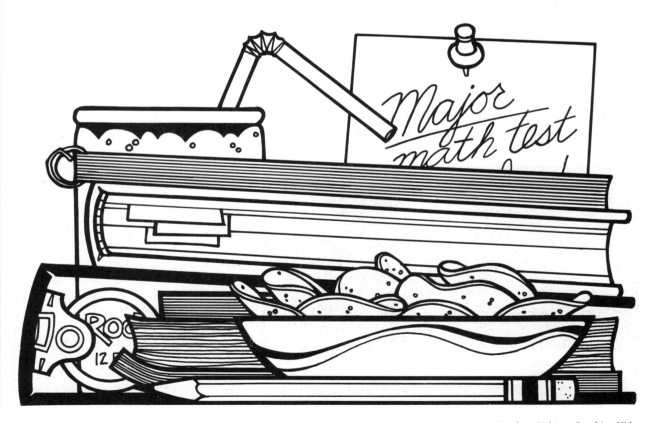

Perseverance Profiles

Select a man or woman you admire for their perseverance. The person you select may be living or deceased, young or old, famous or relatively unknown. You may choose someone on your own or select a person from the following list.

- Susan B. Anthony
- Clara Barton
- Mary McLeod Bethune
- Luther Burbank
- George Washington Carver
- Amelia Earhart
- Thomas Alva Edison
- Medgar Evers
- Benjamin Franklin
- John H. Glenn, Jr.
- Helen Keller

- Martin Luther King, Jr.
- Margaret Mead
- Sandra Day O'Connor
- Paul Revere
- Sally Ride
- John Roosevelt (Jackie) Robinson
- Eleanor Roosevelt
- Maria Tallchief
- Harriet Tubman
- Booker T. Washington
- Charles E. Yeager

Do research to learn more about the life of the person you selected. Find specific examples of how he or she persevered during difficult times. Be sure to find contributions this person made to society. Take thorough notes as you do your research.

Share your findings with your classmates in the form of an oral report where you become the person you selected. Use the word "I" when you present your report. For example, if you selected Amelia Earhart, you might begin your profile like this . . .

My name is Amelia Earhart. I was a famous pilot who . . .

You might even want to dress up as the person you selected. Use props and visual aids to make your oral profile more interesting. The emphasis of your profile should be on how you persevered. What obstacles did you face? How did you overcome them?

Summing Up Perseverance

Complete each statement or question.

Something new I learned about perseverance is _____

_____

_____

I ☐ did reach   ☐ am still reaching for the "perseverance" goals I set for myself.

I hope to work harder to persevere at tasks in the future because _____

_____

_____

One area I still need to work on when it comes to perseverance is _____

_____

_____

When it comes to perseverance, I'm good at _____

_____

_____

STAMINA PATIENCE
STEADFASTNESS
DETERMINATION

PERSEVERANCE

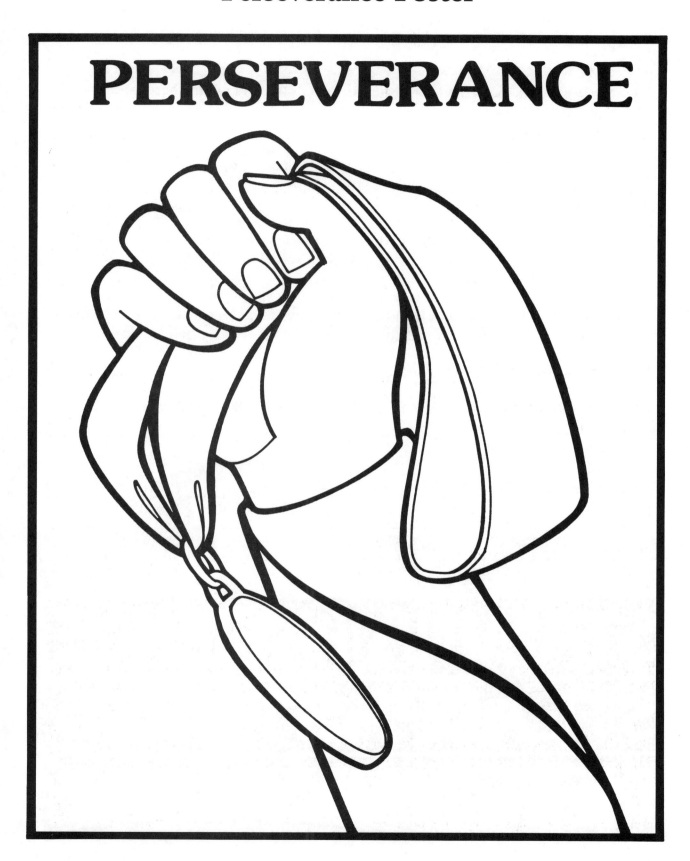

Quotes on Perseverance

- Victory belongs to the most persevering.
  Napoleon Bonaparte

- Many strokes, though with a little axe, hew down and fell the hardest-timber'd oak.
  William Shakespeare—from Henry VI

- The difference between perseverance and obstinacy is that one often comes from a strong will, and the other from a strong won't.
  Henry Ward Beecher

- Perseverance is more prevailing than violence; and many things which cannot be overcome when they are together yield themselves up when taken little by little.
  Plutarch

- There is no failure except in no longer trying. There is no defeat except from within, no really insurmountable barrier save our own inherent weakness of purpose.
  Kin Hubbard

- Consider the postage stamp: its usefulness consists in the ability to stick to one thing till it gets there.
  Josh Billings

- Hitch your wagon to a star.
  Ralph Waldo Emerson

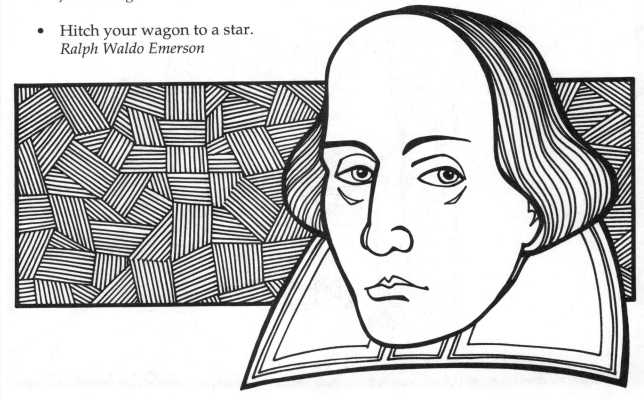

Quotes on Perseverance

- Many a man never fails because he never tries.
  Norman Macewan

- Perseverance is more prevailing than violence; and many things which cannot be overcome when they are together, yield themselves up when taken little by little.
  Plutarch

- To persevere, trusting in what hopes he has, is courage in a man. The coward despairs.
  Euripides

- The person who makes a success of living is the one who sees his goal steadily and aims for it unswervingly. That is dedication.
  Cecil B. DeMille

- It is hard to fail, but it is worse never to have tried to succeed. In this life we get nothing save by effort.
  Theodore Roosevelt

- Many strokes overthrow the tallest oaks.
  John Lyly

- You may be disappointed if you fail, but you are doomed if you don't try.
  Beverly Sills

Follow-Up Activities
Perseverance

- Interview an adult in your family: a parent, grandparent, aunt, uncle, or cousin. Ask him or her to share a story about growing up in his or her generation. Ask this person to tell you about examples of perseverance that he or she remembers about his or her childhood. Then write a short story based on these incidents.

- Write an adventure story about an ordinary boy or girl your age who perseveres to accomplish a great feat, such as climbing a mountain, running a marathon, or sailing around the world. Add illustrations to the final draft of your story.

- Make a perseverance collage by going through old newspapers and magazines and cutting out words and pictures that you think symbolize perseverance. Then arrange and overlap the words and pictures on a poster to display in your class.

- Pick a perseverance project for yourself. Try something you've always wanted to attempt such as learning a new sport, a foreign language, or a new hobby such as painting, sewing, or playing a musical instrument. Stick to your goal for the entire month. Keep a journal and record your feelings about your efforts as you go. Were there times you felt discouraged and thought about giving up? In your journal, describe your ups and downs—your defeats as well as your triumphs. Evaluate your progress at the end of the month and decide if you want to continue or perhaps even add a new goal for the next month.

Chapter 5
Compassion

**kindness, caring;
understanding how another person feels**

Sorry about your throat....

A Letter to Parents

Dear Parents,

This month our class will be learning about the value of **compassion** through class discussions, role-playing, creative writing, and art. We will be learning ways to become more compassionate at home, at school, and in the community.

One of the ways children learn about compassion is through examples they see in their homes. When you as parents get involved in volunteer projects in your community, you send a strong message to your child about caring and compassion. During the course of this unit, take time to talk to your child about what compassion means.

Generate discussions about why it is important to be compassionate and the personal rewards people get when they help others. Pick a project your whole family can participate in to help someone in need in your community so your child learns firsthand about the great feeling that comes from helping others.

Here are other ways you can reinforce the value of compassion with your child:

- Volunteer as a family to help serve at a soup kitchen in your community.

- Ask all members of the family to save their spare change. Keep the coins in a jar your child decorates. Then donate the money to a charitable organization in your community.

- At holiday times such as Hanukkah, Christmas, Kwanzaa, and Thanksgiving, do something nice as a family for those who are less fortunate.

Thanks for working with us in helping to teach your child about the value of **compassion**. Please feel free to visit our class and see what we're doing to learn more about being compassionate.

Sincerely,

What Is Compassion?

In your own words, describe what the word *compassion* means.

_____

_____

_____

_____

Find the word *compassion* in a dictionary and write its definition below.

_____

_____

_____

Describe a time you felt compassion for someone else. What did you do or say?

_____

_____

_____

_____

Describe a time someone treated you compassionately. What did this person do or say?

_____

_____

_____

_____

What Are Examples of Compassion?

You are showing compassion when you . . .

- comfort a friend whose mother has been taken to the hospital

- bring blankets and food to a family in need in your community

- read about a disaster in the newspaper and send a donation to an organization that will help the families

- visit a senior citizen in a nursing home and spend some time with him or her

- volunteer to help out at the Special Olympics

- take action and stop someone who is being cruel to an animal

- bring ice cream to a friend who has had his or her tonsils removed

- can understand why your best friend is depressed about her parent's divorce

- send a donation to help people starving in a foreign country after learning about them on the evening news

- tutor a younger child who is having trouble in school

- are understanding when your dad loses his job

- listen when a close friend confides in you and tells you his or her troubles

What are some other examples of compassion you might find at home, at school, or in your community? List as many examples of compassion as you can.

Teaching Values—Reaching Kids
© The Learning Works, Inc.

Setting Goals for Yourself

Set goals for yourself that involve showing compassion and kindness. List one goal under each heading below. Think about how you can accomplish each goal. Take time to evaluate your goals on a regular basis to see how you're doing.

At Home

At School

To Other People in My Community

To Animals and the Environment

Local Heroes

Newspaper headlines are usually filled with events that grab attention, such as murders, accidents, and other tragedies. But there are also articles telling about boys, girls, men, and women who have done outstanding things to help other people, animals, or their communities.

Go through your local newspaper and find an article about someone who has done something kind for someone else. Bring the article to school and share it with your classmates. Make a classroom bulletin board called "Local Heroes" and post the articles you find over the next several weeks.

"Be Kind to Others" Week

Plan a school-wide "Be Kind to Others" Week. As a class, decide on the following issues:

- How can you let other classes know about this special week: posters, flyers, assemblies?

- What kinds of kind deeds will be recognized?

- How will you share the compassionate things students are doing with the student body?

- How will the students be acknowledged for their kind deeds?

- Can a newsletter be planned to inform parents of the kind things happening at your school?

Come up with questions of your own. Work as a class to solve any problems that might arise as you plan your special week.

Showing You Care

You might not be able to change the world, but you can take small steps in your daily life to treat other people with compassion to make the world a kinder place. Try these acts of kindness . . .

Check in on an elderly neighbor
and offer to run errands or
help with household tasks.

Donate books you no longer read
to a local hospital or shelter
so other kids can enjoy them.

Bake a batch of cookies for a neighbor
or friend who is sick, and make a
get-well card to cheer him or her up.

Volunteer to take care
of a neighbor's pet
while he or she is on vacation.

With your classmates, make a list of other things you can do to make our world a kinder and more compassionate place. List ideas under each heading. Then make plans to implement your favorite ideas as class projects throughout the school year.

- Helping Other Children
- Helping the Elderly
- Helping the Needy
- Helping the Environment
- Helping Our Community

132

Comments on Compassion

Here are some questions for you and your classmates to think about and discuss.

- Do you think people are born with compassion or is it something people learn?

- How can parents teach their children compassion?

- What examples of compassion have you seen?

- Do you think most people in the world are compassionate? Why or why not?

- Is our world today more or less compassionate than in the past?

- What famous people living today do you consider to be compassionate? What have they done to help others?

- The opposite of compassion is cruelty. Have you ever been cruel to someone else? Describe what happened. How did it make you feel?

- Has anyone ever been cruel to you? Describe what happened. How did you feel?

- What can kids do at school to show more compassion to their classmates?

- What can people do to make our world a more compassionate place?

Becoming More Compassionate

When you reach out to help others, a lot of great things happen. You end up meeting new people and developing new friendships. You expand your skills, knowledge, and interests. The more you do for others, the better you become at organizing, planning, and carrying out your ideas. You'll also find that helping other people makes you feel good about yourself.

There are many ways to become a more caring, compassionate person. Here are a few tips.

- **Be a good listener.**
  Pay close attention when others talk to you. Make an effort to really hear what they are saying. Wait until they're finished speaking before responding or giving your opinion.

- **Look people directly in the eye when you speak.**
  When you look at people straight in the eye as you speak, it reflects interest and caring. Don't let your attention drift to other things that are happening around you. Make the person you are talking to feel really important and cared for by the attention you pay to him or her.

- **Look for kids at school who are being left out.**
  Become aware of kids who are excluded from activities at school: during lunch, on the playground, or while doing group projects. Make an extra effort to include these kids in your circle of friends and in your activities.

- **Stick up for someone being teased.**
  Put yourself in the shoes of someone who is being picked on and teased at school. Imagine how he or she feels. Then go to his or her aid. Let the person know you are there to offer support as a friend.

- **Each week, do one nice thing for a friend or family member.**
  Practice makes perfect. The more nice things you do for people, the closer you come to becoming a compassionate person. Bring a book to a friend who is home sick in bed. Make dinner for your family so your mom or dad won't have to cook one night. Bring ice cream to a friend who has had a tooth pulled. Make a "thinking of you" card and send it to a grandparent who lives far away.

What other compassionate things can you think of?

Role-Playing Compassion

When you want to help a person who is in need, it is important to think about what you are trying to accomplish and decide how you can put your plan into action. Role-play the following situation with your classmates. Show the rest of your class what you would do in this situation. Let other teams role-play the same situation and see how many different solutions your class can come up with. Then vote on the idea your class would most like to undertake as a project during the month you are learning about compassion.

You read a newspaper article about starving children in Africa. The article and accompanying pictures of hungry, crying children affects you deeply. At school the next day, you discuss the article with a few of your friends. You come up with a unique plan your whole class can participate in to raise money for these starving children. It makes you feel good to know that even though you can't save the entire world, you can at least take a small step to help kids who are less fortunate than you.

Describe your plan of action and how you plan to implement it. Tell about the various roles your classmates will take on your project as you work towards your goal. Tell how you will research various organizations that provide relief to starving children in Africa and how you will decide on which organization to donate your money to.

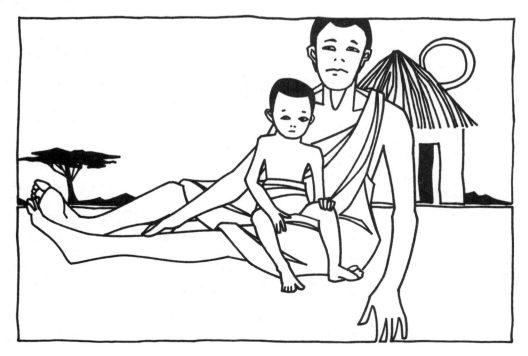

Helping Other Children

One way to show compassion is to volunteer your time to help other children, especially those less fortunate than you. You can work with kids at a child-care center or nursery school, in a kindergarten class at your school or in your neighborhood, at a shelter for the homeless, in an after-school program, or in other places where young children are receiving care.

Here are some ideas for things you can do to help other children.

This is GRONK. He glows in the dark !!

Donate Toys and Games

Look through your closet and check your shelves to find toys and games you have outgrown. Clean and/or repair them and donate them to a facility for young children to play with and enjoy. For a personal touch, add a note with a brief message to a child for each toy you donate.

Tutor a Child

Take time to tutor a child after school or on weekends. Contact shelters, schools, or community organizations that reach out to children. They can help put you in touch with a boy or girl who would benefit from working with you for an hour each week. You could be a tutor for math, grammar, history, music, spelling, reading—whatever you're good at and enjoy.

Tutoring April 12
- practice spelling
- read dinosaur book
- work on map of neighborhood

136

Helping Other Children
continued

Coins for Kids

Collect spare change from your pocket and wallet each day. Ask family members and friends to add to your coin collection. When your container of coins is full, roll the money into change wrappers that are available at most banks. Then take your wrapped change to the bank and ask the teller to give you paper currency in exchange for the rolled coins. Use the money you collected to buy any of the following items that children could use:

- blankets
- children's books
- stuffed animals
- school supplies such as paper or crayons
- cassette tapes
- toys or games

You might wish to first contact an organization to find out what things are most needed.

Tape Your Favorite Book

Create a read-along tape for a youngster who is sick or to give as a gift. All you need is a picture book you've outgrown, a tape recorder, a blank tape, and a small bell. Find a quiet place and time to tape so you won't be interrupted. Read the story slowly, clearly, and with lots of expression as you record it. You will need to ring the bell to let the child know when to turn each page. Include the book as part of your gift so the young child can read along with the tape.

Helping the Elderly

You can show compassion and kindness by doing something nice for a senior citizen. However, before you pick a project or begin, here are a few things to keep in mind.

- Some older people tire easily and need to take naps during the day. If you plan to visit a senior citizen in a nursing home or retirement facility, be sure to find out the best time for your visit.

- If you plan to take food when you visit, make sure you know about any dietary restrictions or special needs.

- Always call to set up an appointment time before going to visit an elderly person in a retirement home or nursing home. Don't promise to visit and then fail to show up. If your plans change and you can't make your visit as planned, be sure to call, let the person know, and reschedule your visit so he or she won't be disappointed.

- Everyone loves surprises. Each time you visit, bring something special to show your friend—a school or scout project you are working on, shells you've collected, or a picture of yourself. These can be great conversation starters.

Here are some ideas for projects you can do with an elderly person you visit in a nursing home, rehabilitation center, retirement community, convalescent hospital, or recreation department.

Write a Letter

Volunteer to be a secretary for an elderly person who has difficulty writing. Ask if the person would like to dictate a letter to a family member or friend while you write for him or her. When you are finished writing the letter, read it aloud to make sure that it is accurate.

Address the envelope, donate a stamp, and mail the letter for your senior friend.

Helping the Elderly
continued

Be a Pen Pal

Be a pen pal to a senior citizen. When you send a card, letter, or cheery note to a senior citizen, it makes him or her feel cared about and brightens the person's day. When you write, you can also send along a poem, original art work, or a short story you've written. Send a card to your pen pal on his or her birthday, on special occasions, or just to say "hello" and let the person know you care.

Read to a Senior

Many elderly people have difficulty reading the small print in newspapers and books because their eyesight is failing. While there are books with large type available in libraries, not everyone has easy access to them. Volunteer your time to read aloud to a senior citizen from a magazine, a book, a local newspaper, or a collection of poetry. This is a great way for you to practice your oral reading skills while bringing pleasure to someone who loves to read but can't.

Play a Game

Most people enjoy playing games. It's a good way to get to know someone better and adds variety and excitement for a senior citizen who spends a lot of time alone. Plan a visit to a nursing home, a retirement home, or a hospital and challenge a senior citizen to a game of chess, cards, or checkers. Another idea is to bring along your favorite board game to play together.

Helping People in Need

There are many times and situations in your community where you can show compassion and provide help for other people. Anyone can find themselves in need at one time or another. Some people have had very difficult lives and could use a helping hand. Some of these people may have lost their jobs; others may be homeless. Some people may be ill or may have a family member who is suffering from a chronic illness. Natural disasters such as fires, earthquakes, floods, or hurricanes may unexpectedly leave an individual or family homeless or stranded without any personal possessions. Here are a few suggestions for things you can do in your neighborhood or community to show compassion to people in need.

Donate Clothes

Donate clothes you and other family members have outgrown to a shelter or to a program that helps homeless people. You can even organize a "Clean Your Closet Week" with your classmates and donate all the clothes collected to help people in need.

To add a warm, personal touch to your donation, pick one article of clothing from among those you are donating. Write a short note telling about something special that happened while you were wearing this article of clothing—such as scoring the winning goal for your soccer team. Attach your note to the article of clothing.

Share a Celebration

Start a new tradition in your family. At your next birthday party, ask each guest to bring a wrapped gift for a person in need. It could be a gift of nonperishable food, a book, a household item, clothing, a bath item, or a new toy. You get the fun of unwrapping the gifts and the good feeling that comes from donating them to an agency that helps people in need. Each family member can make this idea a part of his or her next birthday or any gift-giving celebration.

Helping People in Need
continued

Help After a Disaster

Volunteer your time following a natural disaster such as a mudslide, tornado, an earthquake, hurricane, or flood. You can help by making and putting up signs to help people find lost pets, collecting and distributing blankets, making sandwiches for rescue workers and volunteers, or by raising money to help a family in your community. There are many other ways you can show you care and can make a difference to other people during a time of need.

Go On a Scavenger Hunt for Food

At your next birthday party, reach out to help people in need by organizing a food scavenger hunt. Divide your guests into teams of three or four players. Give each team grocery bags and a list of items to find as they go from house to house in your neighborhood. Be sure an adult is along to supervise each group.

Food items on your list can include the names of specific types of soups such as tomato, vegetable, or mushroom. Include canned vegetables such as beets, carrots, and peas. You can also include types of canned fruit, baby food, jelly, etc. on your list. Ask each team to go to a different area to avoid several teams asking for food at the same house. Team members should be told not to go into anyone's house. Be sure they explain that they are collecting the food to help people in need. Ask your guests to meet back at your house in thirty minutes. Then give a prize to the team that brings back the most food. Donate all the food you and your guests collect to an agency or organization that distributes food to families needing assistance.

Helping Animals

Working as a class, pick a project you can do to show compassion to an animal. There are many people, places, and organizations you can contact that will give you guidance and answer questions you might have. Start by talking to veterinarians, park rangers, the staff of animal shelters, or marine biologists. Places you can visit for information include your local library, zoo, animal shelter, wildlife refuge, nature center, pet store, or natural history museum. Also check your local telephone directory for the names and phone numbers of organizations such as the Humane Society of the United States, the National Wildlife Federation, the National Audubon Society, or the American Society for the Prevention of Cruelty to Animals.

Brainstorm different project ideas with your classmates. Then have your class pick its favorite and plan how to organize what needs to be done to reach your goals. For example, you could make toys for pets in a neighborhood animal shelter. Several ideas are described on page 143. You could also make posters for pet shops or animal shelters reminding people to have their pets spayed or neutered so unwanted cats and dogs do not have to be destroyed. You might also want to prepare a skit on pet care and perform it for younger students at your school.

Helping Animals

One way to show compassion for pets is to make a simple toy for an animal in your classroom, in an animal shelter, or at home. Here are a few ideas to get you going:

Turn paper grocery bags into cat toys. Cut holes in the sides for the cats to peek through or reach through and decorate the bags with marking pens.

Glue ice cream sticks to a piece of cardboard to make a ladder for a hamster.

Make a rattle for a rabbit by placing a few buttons or small pebbles inside a juice can and taping it shut.

Tie a tennis ball inside an old sock for tossing and tugging games.

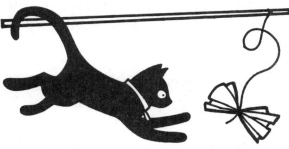

Use a stick, a string, and a piece of paper to make a "fishing pole" for a pet kitty. Waxed paper and cellophane are good noisemakers.

Use round oatmeal boxes and cardboard tubes to make tunnels for little critters.

Helping Your Community

Volunteer to do something nice for the community in which you live. There are many organizations in your community that could use your help. Check in your local telephone directory for places such as senior centers, libraries, hospitals, or recreation departments that could use your assistance. Organizations such as family service agencies, community service organizations, the American Red Cross, Girls Incorporated, Camp Fire Boys and Girls, Boy Scouts and Girl Scouts can always use your help if you have the time to volunteer. Here are some ideas for ways to get involved and to help.

Stuff Envelopes

Nonprofit organizations in your community usually do several mailings a year to inform citizens of their goals and objectives or to solicit funds for their causes. Choose an organization in your community you'd like to help and volunteer to stuff envelopes. The preparation of these mailings is very time consuming, and many organizations are short-handed. They will truly appreciate the time and help you donate.

Help Serve Food

Volunteer with your classmates to help serve food at a community shelter. Make this an ongoing classroom project—not just at holiday time. After you help serve the meal, take time to talk and play with younger children at the facility. You might want to bring along a favorite book or game to share.

144

Helping Your Community
continued

Plan an Appreciation Day

Plan a special day to show your appreciation for people who have made your community a better place in which to live. You might choose to honor a librarian, a school crossing guard, a police officer, a fire fighter, or your school principal. On Appreciation Day, do something special for the people you selected. You might want to bake some cookies or give them a homemade gift. Include a thank-you card to let each person know how much you appreciate all he or she has done for your community.

Here are the names and addresses of several national organizations that serve communities everywhere. Check your local telephone directory to see if there is an office in your area. If there isn't, contact the central office for the nearest location.

American Red Cross
430 17th Street N.W.
Washington, D.C. 20006

Children's Quilt Project
1478 University Avenue, Suite 186
Berkeley, CA 94702

Goodwill Industries International, Inc.
9200 Rockville Pike
Bethesda, MD 20814

Special Olympics International
1325 G. Street N.W., Suite 500
Washington, D.C. 20005-3104

United Way of America
701 North Fairfax Street
Alexandria, VA 22314

Youth Services of America
1101 15th Street, N.W., Suite 200
Washington, D.C. 20005

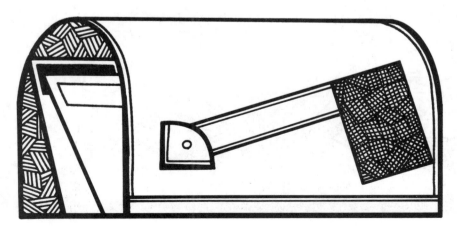

Helping the Environment

When you take steps to protect the environment, you help create a cleaner and safer world for everyone. Here are some ideas for projects you and your class-mates can do to help the environment. Have fun coming up with your own ideas to implement. You **can** make a difference!

Help Save a Rain Forest

Contact The Nature Conservancy to find out more about the "adopt-an-acre" program. By donating money, you can help them purchase and protect rain forest land. Brainstorm ways you and your classmates can raise money such as having a bake sale, a talent show, or an aluminum can drive.

The Nature Conservancy
1815 N. Lynn Street
Arlington, VA 22209

Adopt a Stream

As a class, adopt a stream in your community. Take steps to protect it from pollution. For example, you might pick up litter alongside the stream so that it will not fall into the water. You might also look for possible sources of pollution and report any you find to your teacher or adults who can decide what should be done. Be sure the stream you adopt is located on public property and that you are not trespassing on private property. For more information, write to:

Save Our Streams
The Izaak Walton League of America
1401 Wilson Boulevard—Level B
Arlington, VA 22209

146

A Picture of Compassion

What picture comes to mind when you think of the word *compassion*? In the frame below, draw a picture that you feel best describes compassion. You can use crayons, felt-tipped markers, or watercolors to color your picture.

Summing Up Compassion

Complete each statement or question.

Something new I learned about compassion is _____

_____

_____

_____

_____

Did you reach the "compassion" goals you set for yourself? Give examples of how you are moving toward them or have accomplished them.

_____

_____

_____

_____

_____

_____

_____

One area I still need to work on when it comes to compassion is _____

_____

_____

_____

Quotes on Compassion and Kindness

- Kindness gives birth to kindness.
Sophocles

- A bone to the dog is not charity. Charity is the bone shared with the dog when you are just as hungry as the dog.
Jack London

- Human kindness has never weakened the stamina or softened the fiber of a free people. A nation does not have to be cruel in order to be tough.
Franklin Delano Roosevelt

- A kind heart is a foundation of gladness, making everything in its vicinity freshen into smiles.
Washington Irving

- You cannot do a kindness too soon, for you never know how soon it will be too late.
Ralph Waldo Emerson

- Be nice to people on your way up because you'll meet them on your way down.
Wilson Mizner

- Wherever there is a human being, there is an opportunity for a kindness.
Seneca

- I expect to pass through life but once. If, therefore, there can be any kindness I can show, or any good things I can do for any fellow being, let me do it now and not defer or neglect it, as I shall not pass this way again.
William Penn

- I feel that the greatest reward for doing is the opportunity to do more.
Jonas Salk

150

Quotes on Compassion and Kindness

- Kindness in words creates confidence. Kindness in thinking creates profoundness. Kindness in giving creates love.
  Lao-tzu

- Kindness is a language which the deaf can hear and the blind can read.
  Mark Twain

- The only ones among you who will be really happy are those who have sought and found how to serve.
  Albert Schweitzer

- The things to do are the things that need doing that you see need to be done and that no one else seems to see need to be done.
  R. Buckminster Fuller

- In spite of everything, I still believe that people are good at heart.
  Anne Frank

- To give life a meaning, one must have a purpose larger than one's self.
  Will Durant

- It is one of the beautiful compensations of this life that no one can sincerely try to help another without helping himself.
  Charles Dudley Warner

- The best portion of a good man's life—his little, nameless, unremembered acts of kindness and love.
  William Wordsworth

- The entire value of a kind deed depends on the love that inspires it.
  the *Talmud*

Teacher Follow-Up Activities
Compassion

- Create a class banner with the theme of compassion. Give each student a piece of material and ask him or her to design a square that reflects compassion. The emphasis could be on having compassion for other people, for animals, for the environment, etc. Ask the students to plan their design on scratch paper first, and then do their final version using felt or other material. Solicit the help of a parent who sews to stitch the final squares of the banner together. You can donate the banner to a senior citizen home, hospital, or charitable organization, or raffle it off at a PTA meeting to raise money for a needy charity.

- Organize a class sing-along at a convalescent hospital, a nursery school, a community center, a shopping mall, a homeless shelter, or a senior citizen center. Have your students make a sing-along program with the words to popular tunes, and distribute copies to participants. If you have a music teacher at your school, perhaps he or she can help you organize a program. This is a great class activity to do not only at holiday times but any time during the school year!

- At holiday time, ask your students to make original greeting cards for people in hospitals, retirement homes, or convalescent facilities. As a special treat, have your students include original poems or short stories to give with the greeting cards.

- Take time each Friday to go around the class and have students share some of the kind, compassionate things they have done for family members, classmates, friends, relatives, neighbors, or animals or that they have observed others doing. Then make a bulletin board in your class entitled "Our Class Cares." Post descriptions of these compassionate things your students have done for others during the week.

Chapter 6
Responsibility

trustworthiness; accountability

A Letter to Parents

Dear Parents,

This month our class will be learning about the value of **responsibility** at home, at school, with friends, and in the community. We'll learn about obeying rules, acting responsibly, being responsible for our own behavior, and taking steps to make responsible decisions. Through class discussions, role-playing, creative writing, and art projects, we will learn ways we can become more responsible people.

During the course of this unit, take time to talk to your child about what responsibility means. Tell him or her about your own experiences involving responsibility on your job or at home. Explain some of the tasks you are required to do on a daily basis, how you work as a team with other people, and how you've grown and become more responsible.

Give your child specific responsibilities around the house and discuss the importance of each family member pitching in to make the family unit run smoothly. Have your child think through the consequences of what would happen if no one did the laundry, took out the garbage, fixed meals, or earned money to pay the rent or mortgage.

Here are other ways you can reinforce the value of responsibility with your child:

- Give your child hypothetical situations dealing with being responsible. Here are a few examples:

    - You forget to do an important class assignment.

    - You find a library book on a park bench.

    - A friend wants you to try smoking a cigarette with her.

Thank you for working with us to help teach your child about the value of **responsibility**. Please feel free to visit our class and see what we're doing to learn more about being responsible.

Sincerely,

Teaching Values—Reaching Kids
© The Learning Works, Inc.

What is Responsibility?

In your own words, describe what the word *responsibility* means.

_____

_____

_____

_____

Find the word *responsibility* in a dictionary and write its definition below.

_____

_____

_____

Describe a time when you acted responsibly.

_____

_____

_____

_____

_____

Describe a time when you were not very responsible.

_____

_____

_____

_____

What Are Examples of Being Responsible?

You are being responsible when you . . .

- complete your chores at home without being constantly reminded

- take good care of your personal possessions

- come home from a party within the curfew time your mom or dad has set

- call your parents if you are going to be late coming home so they won't be worried

- eat healthy food, get plenty of exercise, and take good care of yourself

- remember to bring your jacket home from soccer practice so it doesn't get lost

- take care of your lunch money and don't lose it on the playground

- keep a promise you made to a friend

- frequently check on the kids you are baby-sitting when they are asleep

- put part of your allowance into a savings account instead of spending it all

- complete your school assignments on time and to the best of your ability

- take care of your pet and make sure it has food and fresh water

What are other examples of responsible behavior at home or at school?

Setting Goals for Responsibility

Set goals to help yourself become a more responsible person. List one goal under each heading below. Think about how you can achieve each goal. Take time to evaluate your goals on a regular basis to see how you're doing.

Being More Responsible at Home

Being More Responsible at School

Being More Responsible to My Friends

Being Responsible at Home

What responsibilities and obligations do you have at home? Give short responses for each of the following situations:

- jobs and chores to do around the house:

- allowance and saving money:

- curfews:

- completing your homework:

- brothers and sisters:

- pets:

- possessions such as clothing, computers, and sports equipment:

- meeting deadlines:

- sports teams or clubs you belong to:

Being Responsible at Home

What would you do in each of these situations? With your classmates, discuss what the most responsible solutions would be.

Your dad wants you to spend your winter break visiting your grandparents who live in Florida. You want to stay home and have time to visit with your friends. Your dad feels you have a responsibility and obligation to spend time with your grandparents whom you hardly ever see.

While practicing your golf swing in your front yard, you hit the ball too hard and it crashes through the windshield of a neighbor's car. No one sees the incident or notices as you retrieve your ball.

Your bedroom look like a pig sty. The mess doesn't bother you, but it drives your parents crazy. Since it's your room you feel you should be able to keep it any way you want. Your mom and dad insist you keep it clean so you learn how to be responsible for your belongings.

Since your mom works full time, she expects you go get dinner started most weekday nights. You're tired when you come home from school, have homework to do, and want time to talk on the phone with your friends. You don't think you should be responsible for preparing dinners.

Responsibilities at School

On a separate piece of paper, write short answers for each of the following questions.

- As you grow and mature, your teachers give you more and more responsibilities at school. List three responsibilities you now have at school that you didn't have three years ago.

- How do these responsibilities help you grow as a person and prepare you for the future?

- Describe a time you were given an important school assignment or project to do. Did you work alone or in a small group? Did you accomplish everything you set out to do? Did you meet your deadline? How did you feel about the work you did? What did you learn from this experience?

- Describe a time you did **not** follow through on a school assignment or project. What was the outcome of not meeting your responsibilities? How did you feel? What did you learn from this experience?

- Describe a time when you did not take responsibility for your actions. For example, perhaps you let someone else take the blame for something you did. How did you feel? What would you differently next time if you were in the same situation?

- Describe a time you let a classmate down because you didn't meet your responsibilities. How did your friend handle this incident? How did you feel? What did you learn from this experience?

- Describe a time a classmate let you down because he or she wasn't acting responsibly. How did this incident make you feel? What did you say to your friend? What was his or her reaction? What did you learn from this experience?

Teaching Values—Reaching Kids
© The Learning Works, Inc.

A Responsibility Survey

Complete the following survey about responsibility at school.
Check the appropriate box for each item.

	always	sometimes	never
get to school on time			
complete and turn in my classwork			
complete and turn in my homework			
remember to bring my lunch or lunch money from home			
do my fair share when working in small groups on classroom projects			
admit it is my fault when I do something wrong at school			
keep my desk at school neat and well organized			
keep my school notebook neat and well organized			
follow and obey school rules in the classroom and on the playground			

Obeying the Rules

Rules, rules, rules! It seems like there are rules for almost every aspect of your life. Your parents have rules for you to follow at home, your school has rules for the classroom and playground, your coach expects you to follow rules of play for the sports you participate in, and even your community has rules for you to obey when riding your bike, crossing the street, or riding in a car.

Stop for a minute to think about the responsibility of following rules. In your class, take time to discuss each of the following questions.

1. Why are rules necessary at home, in the classroom, in sports, and in the community?

2. How are different rules enforced?

3. Why do you think some people refuse to obey rules?

4. What happens when people don't follow the rules?

5. How do kids your age learn to be responsible for obeying rules?

Pick one of the following situations and describe some rules a responsible person would follow:

- while browsing on the Internet
- at a school assembly
- at a baseball game
- in church or synagogue
- while eating dinner at a fancy restaurant
- while at an amusement park
- at the library
- during a final exam at school
- while visiting relatives in their home
- while riding your bicycle or rollerblading

Responsibilities in Your Community

Whether you live in the country, in a busy city, on a farm, or in the suburbs, as a member of your community you have certain responsibilities.

On a separate piece of paper, design a poster to illustrate how members of a community can act more responsibly. After you design your poster, color it with crayons, paints, or felt-tipped markers. As a class, display your posters in your school office or cafeteria for others to share. Select one of the following themes or come up with your own.

- Clean Up Litter
- Drive Safely
- Help Your Neighbors
- Let's Recycle
- Stop Vandalism
- Protect Your Pets
- Beautify Our Community

Responsible Behavior

You are responsible for your own behavior. If you use poor judgment in the things you do, you have to pay the consequences. Sometimes you are faced with tricky situations when it comes to your behavior. Many choices that are easy for you to make when you are alone become much more difficult and complicated when friends are involved. On a separate sheet of paper, describe what you would do in each of the following situations. Describe the consequences of both responsible and irresponsible behavior.

While in a drugstore, a friend dares you to steal a candy bar. Your friend does it all the time and has never been caught. You're broke and a candy bar sounds pretty good.

You are spending the night at a friend's house. His parents are out for the evening. Your friend tells you his parents have a gun hidden in the house and he wants to show it to you.

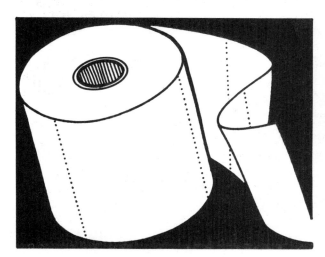

While at a slumber party, someone suggests sneaking out and toilet-papering a neighbor's house. Everyone laughs and decides it would be a lot of fun—everyone but you.

You borrow a friend's bike while yours is being repaired. While riding it to the store, you hit a rock and fall. You're bruised—but even worse, the bike frame is bent out of shape and the paint is scraped.

Teaching Values—Reaching Kids
© The Learning Works, Inc.

Responsible Behavior
continued

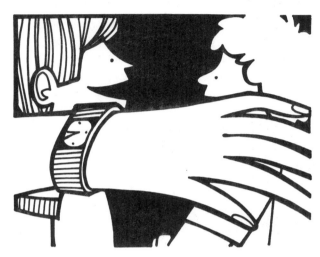

You've promised your parents you'll be home from a party at 9:00 because you have an important playoff game early the next morning. The party is still in full swing at 8:45. None of the other kids have left and you want to stay at the party until everyone else goes home.

You've had about all you can take from an older kid who is always picking on you, teasing you, and giving you a hard time. You've warned him that the next time he bothers you, you're going to put him in his place. On the playground during recess, you see him headed your way and you sense there's going to be trouble.

Some classmates offer you a cigarette on the way home after school. On the one hand, you know it's not healthy and you're scared to try it. But on the other hand, you don't know how to say no to your classmates without looking foolish.

You find a wallet full of credit cards and money in the parking lot of a large shopping mall. There is an identification card with the owner's name, address, and telephone number.

Steps to Making Responsible Decisions

As you grow older, you'll have the responsibility of making more and more decisions for yourself—from simple choices such as which clothes to buy or what classes to sign up for to more serious decisions such as which college to go to, what career path to follow, if and when to marry, where to settle down, etc. There are steps you can take to help you make more responsible decisions and choices.

Making Decisions

1. Define your goal. Think about what it is you actually want in the long run.

2. Explore all the choices and options open to you.

3. Gather information and facts. If appropriate, talk to knowledgeable people.

4. Write down arguments for and against each choice. Seeing the pros and cons in writing will help you clarify your decision.

5. Take time to think through the consequences of each of your choices.

6. Make your decision.

Think of an important decision you have to make. Let's see how you can apply the steps listed above to help you reach a responsible decision. (If you can't think of a decision you have to make, select a choice you had to make over this past year.) On a separate piece of paper, go through each step above and describe how you could apply each of these steps to reach your decision.

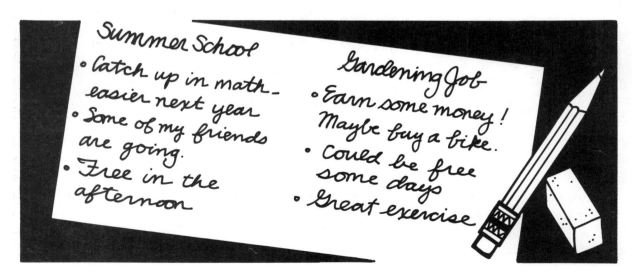

Responsibility in the News

Recently, there was a newspaper article about an armored car that overturned on a city street in a very poor neighborhood. Money went flying in all directions. Some of the people who witnessed the accident went scurrying to gather any money they could find. Later, authorities went door-to-door asking residents to return any money they took. Only two people returned the money they found. One was a mother of two small children. She told reporters that even though she could use the money, she felt it was her responsibility to return the money since it didn't belong to her. She said she wanted to set a good example for her two young children and that returning the money was the right thing to do.

Write a newspaper article about someone in your community who acts responsibly. Draw his or her picture in the box. Think of a catchy headline for your human interest story about responsibility.

You're the Boss

Pretend that you are the boss in each of the following situations. It is up to you to hire the most responsible possible person for each job. Briefly describe the qualities you would look for in prospective applicants.

For example, if you were going to hire a baby-sitter for your six-year-old child, you would want a person who:

- was punctual

- could handle an emergency if one should arise

- would spend quality time with your child, not just sit in front of the television while your child played

- would not be on the telephone all night

- would not invite his or her friends over to your house while baby-sitting

- would straighten up any messes made in your house while you were gone

- would respect your personal belongings

All of the items above reflect a person who is responsible—the kind of person you would trust with the well-being of your child.

List the five most important qualities for each of these positions if you were the boss and were hiring a new:

doctor

1. _____
2. _____
3. _____
4. _____
5. _____

You're the Boss

teacher

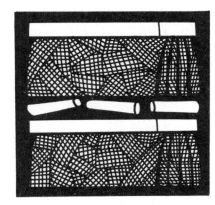

1. _____
2. _____
3. _____
4. _____
5. _____

school bus driver

1. _____
2. _____
3. _____
4. _____
5. _____

soccer coach

1. _____
2. _____
3. _____
4. _____
5. _____

Responsibility Interviews

The responsibilities you have today are probably very different from those your grandmother or grandfather had when she or he was your age. Interview one of your grandparents. If they don't live in the same city as you, call, write, fax, or e-mail the following questions for them to answer. (Be sure to add some of your own questions, too.) If a grandparent is not available, interview your mom, dad, aunt, uncle, or other relative.

Questionnaire

1. When you were my age, what chores were you responsible for at home?

2. Did you get an allowance? If so, how much did you receive each week?

3. What did you spend your allowance on?

4. Were you able to save any of your allowance?

5. Did you have pets as a child? Were you responsible for them in any way?

6. Did you have brothers or sisters? Were they older or younger than you? In what ways were you responsible for them while growing up?

7. In what ways were you involved in your elementary school?

8. Did you belong to any school clubs or organizations?

9. Were you involved in scouting? If so, what rules did you have to follow?

10. What was your first paying job?

11. What were your responsibilities on the job?

12. What salary were you paid for your first job?

13. How did you teach your children about responsibility?

14. Do you think kids today are more or less responsible than kids were when you were growing up?

15. In your lifetime, what have you learned about responsibility that you think is important for me to know?

When the questionnaire is complete, write a summary of your interview findings. Describe the things you were surprised to learn about the person you interviewed.

Role-Playing Responsibility

Think about what you would do in each of the following situations. Then role-play the situation with several of your classmates. Show the rest of your class how you would solve each problem responsibly.

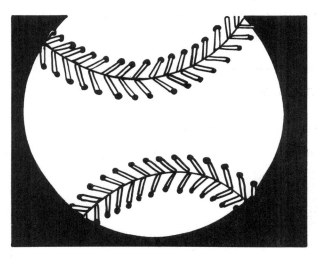

You promised your mom that you would baby-sit your younger brother after school. But when you get home from school, some friends call and ask you to go with them to play ball.

You and a friend are wrestling in his living room. All of a sudden, you are thrown against a table and knock over his mother's expensive crystal vase.

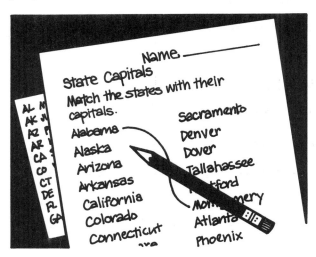

You see a friend cheat during an important exam. Although you feel a certain amount of loyalty to your friend, you also consider how hard you studied for this test, how this person's cheating affects everyone in your class, and what your responsibilities are in this situation.

Your class is planning a surprise party for your teacher's birthday. As class president, it is your responsibility to see that everything runs smoothly. You find out that several committees haven't followed through to complete the work they were supposed to do for the party.

Design a Banner

Design a banner about responsibility to hang in your school cafeteria or front office. Think of a catchy theme, slogan, or saying that will help inspire other kids at school to be responsible students. Add illustrations to your banner and color it with felt-tipped markers, crayons, or paint.

HAVE YOU BEEN A RESPONSIBLE PERSON TODAY?

Be a responsible Mountain View Student . . .
Please help keep our cafeteria clean!

You are responsible for your own behavior at school. Make yourself proud!

172

Summing Up Responsibility

Complete each statement or question.

Something new I learned about responsibility is _____

_____

_____

_____

Did you reach the "responsibility" goals you set for yourself? Give examples of how you are moving toward them or have accomplished them.

_____

_____

_____

_____

_____

Here are some things I still need to work on when it comes to responsibility:

• at home

• at school

• socially

• in my community

• in sports

Quotes on Responsibility

- Responsibility educates.
  Wendell Phillips

- The price of greatness is responsibility.
  Winston Churchill

- Every human being has a work to carry on within, duties to perform abroad, influence to exert, which are peculiarly his, and which no conscience but his own can teach.
  William Ellery Channing

- No man was ever endowed with a right without being at the same time saddled with a responsibility.
  Gerald W. Johnson

- Man is still responsible. He must turn the alloy of modern experience into the steel of mastery and character. His success lies not with the stars but with himself. He must carry on the fight of self-correction and discipline.
  Frank Curtis Williams

Quotes on Responsibility

- Few things help an individual more than to place responsibility upon him and to let him know that you trust him.
  Booker T. Washington

- Man must cease attributing his problems to his environment and learn again to exercise his will—his personal responsibilities in the realm of faith and morals.
  Albert Schweitzer

- The ability to accept responsibility is the measure of the man.
  Roy L. Smith

- How wonderful it is that nobody need wait a single moment before starting to improve the world.
  Anne Frank

- We are all of us fellow passengers on the same planet, and we are all of us equally responsible for the happiness and well-being of the world in which we happen to live.
  Hendrik Willem Van Loon

Student Follow-Up Activities
Responsibility

- Write a poem with responsibility as the theme. Your poem does not have to rhyme.

- As a class, discuss rules for responsible playground behavior. Then summarize your findings and make colorful posters to display at school.

- Work in small groups and write humorous skits about responsibility. Take turns performing your skits for your classmates. Vote on the skits the class enjoyed the most. Perform the favorite skits for other classes as part of a school assembly.

- What are ways you can take responsibility for keeping your bedroom neat, organized, and safe? As a class, brainstorm ideas that you feel are important. Here are some examples to get you started:

    - Pick up small toys your younger brother or sister might put in his or her mouth and choke on.

    - Keep desk and dresser drawers closed so you don't bump into them and hurt yourself, especially at night when it's dark.

    - Keep sharp supplies such as scissors or pens out of the reach of younger brothers or sisters who might wander into your room.

    - Hang your clothes on hangers instead of leaving them on the floor.

    - Place dirty clothes in the hamper.

When your class has completed its list, have fun putting your ideas into a song. Select a simple, popular tune that everyone is familiar with, such as "She'll be Coming Around the Mountain" or "Mary Had a Little Lamb." You might consider dividing into smaller groups, and have each group make up a song for a each idea you brainstormed.

Teacher Follow-Up Activities
Responsibility

- Since many of your students probably ride their bikes to school, invite a police officer to your class to talk about bike safety and responsible bike use. Have your guest review rules of the road and safety tips.

- Another guest you could invite to your class is a representative from the Humane Society. Ask him or her to speak about responsible care of pets such as cats, dogs, birds, hamsters, rabbits, and fish.

- At the beginning of the school year or new semester, ask your students to help make up guidelines for responsible class behavior. By making them a part of the process of establishing the rules, they will feel more responsible for making sure they are carried out. Make a poster outlining the most important rules the class decides on for the year. Take time to evaluate the guidelines set by the class and to add new ones as the need arises.

- Ask your students to work with a partner to write and illustrate a book about responsibility for a young child at your school.

- Make a classroom bulletin board featuring people who have shown outstanding responsibility in their careers. Select people from the fields of politics, education, finance, science, health, sports, and the arts. Ask your students to take turns adding the names, pictures, and stories of other people they discover in newspaper and magazine articles.

Chapter 7
Courage

mental or moral strength
to withstand difficulty, fear, or danger

A Letter to Parents

Dear Parents,

This month our class will be learning about the value of **courage** through discussions, role-playing, creative writing, and art. We will be learning about courage at school and in social situations. We'll learn about the courage it takes to say "no" and how to resist peer pressure. Through class discussions and role-playing, we will practice handling in a variety of situations. We'll also study the lives of famous men and women who have displayed great courage in their lives—people such as Rosa Parks; Helen Keller; Martin Luther King, Jr.; Ryan White; and others.

Whenever possible, take time to talk to your child about courage. Discuss incidents from your own childhood involving courage. Talk about hard decisions you have made in your life and the courage it took on your part. Describe how you felt and how you might have handled things differently. Talk about your heroes and why you admire them. Talking about your own experiences and feelings will help your child talk more easily about his or her feelings.

Here are other ways you can reinforce the value of courage with your child:

- Give your child hypothetical situations dealing with courage to see how he or she would handle each situation. For example, what would your child do if he or she were confronted by a bully on the school playground? Would he or she go to the aid of a friend in danger? What precautions would he or she take?

- As a family, read books that deal with the value of courage. Ask your librarian for suggested novels dealing with the theme of courage or biographies of famous men and women of courage.

Thank you for being our partner in helping to teach your child about the value of **courage**. Please feel free to visit our class and see what we're doing to learn more about courage.

Sincerely,

What is Courage?

In your own words, describe what the word *courage* means.

_____

_____

_____

_____

Find the word *courage* in the dictionary and write its definition below.

_____

_____

_____

Making an attempt to rescue a drowning child is an example of physical courage. What are some other examples of physical courage?

_____

_____

_____

_____

For a person with stage fright, trying out for a part in the school play is an example of emotional courage. What are other examples of emotional courage?

_____

_____

_____

_____

What Are Examples of Courage?

You are being courageous when you . . .

- ride in an elevator even though you have a fear of small, closed-in places
- confront a bully on the playground in defense of a younger child
- are blind but still take swimming lessons
- apologize to someone after you realize you've made a mistake
- stand up for your beliefs even though your views are different from other people
- go to the rescue of someone in trouble
- refuse a cigarette that's offered to you at a party even though most of the kids who are there are smoking
- introduce yourself at a party to a group of people you don't know
- say "hello" to a child who has no friends at school
- select a difficult piece to play for a piano recital when you could have chosen an easier piece you were already familiar with
- play basketball even though you use a wheelchair
- like someone who is not very popular
- enter a poetry contest for the first time
- say "no" to something you know is wrong

What are other examples of courage?

Setting Goals for Yourself

Set goals for yourself that involve acting with courage. List one goal under each heading below. Think about how you can accomplish each goal. You might start with the things you are afraid of and decide how you could overcome these fears. For example, if you are afraid of taking tests and get very nervous before important exams, one of your goals might be to take better notes, get more organized, or start studying earlier rather than waiting until the last minute to review. If you are afraid of earthquakes, you might read to learn more about ways to prepare for and protect yourself during this type of natural disaster.

Showing Courage at Home

Showing Courage at School

Showing Courage in Social Situations

Showing Courage in My Community

Questions About Courage

Courage means standing up for something you believe in. An act of courage usually benefits another person or a group of people, for example, dedicating your life to finding a cure for a disease, working for world peace, or helping to clean up the environment. Doing courageous things for others makes you feel good about yourself. Your own self-respect is raised when you help others and act courageously.

On a separate piece of paper, write a brief answer to each question about courage. Then have a class discussion and share your responses with your classmates.

- Do you think courage is something that can be learned, or are people born with courage?

- Can you have self-respect without courage?

- Does courage always involve taking risks?

- How have acts of courage affected our past?

- Why is courage admired?

- When are acts of courage necessary and important?

- How can acts of courage by a person or group of people make others aware of an existing problem?

- What are examples of physical courage?

- What are example of moral courage?

- How can people learn to overcome their fears and act courageously?

Thinking About Courage

It takes a lot of courage to stand up for the things you believe in, especially when you stand alone on an issue. On a separate piece of paper, write about and describe what you would do if you found yourself in each of these situations.

Your mom, dad, and older brother want to buy a purebred dog from a breeder. You think your family should adopt a dog from the local animal shelter. Describe how you would try to get them to see your point of view.

On an outing with your friends, you are the only one who doesn't want to do something because you believe it is wrong. Describe how you resist peer pressure and keep your self-respect.

On a separate piece of paper, describe a real-life incident where you showed courage and stood up for something you truly believed in. Answer each of the following questions:

- What was the main issue?

- What stand did you take? Why?

- How did you make your views known to the other people involved?

- How did the other people feel?

- What actions did you take?

- What was the outcome?

- What would you do differently next time?

- How did you feel?

- What did you learn from this experience?

Moral Courage

Steve refuses to experiment with drugs even though kids at school tease him and call him chicken.

Jenny admits to her teacher that she cheated on her history exam.

On the school playground, Juanita sticks up for her best friend when a group of girls tease and make fun of her friend.

These are just a few examples of moral courage. Moral courage helps you respect yourself as a person and respect the rights of others. Answer the following questions:

- What are some *synonyms* (words that have similar meanings) for the word **courage**?

_____   _____

_____   _____

- What are some *antonyms* (words that have opposite meanings) of the word **courage**?

_____   _____

_____   _____

GUTS ☐☐☐☐☐ GRIT ☐☐☐☐ SPUNK
☐☐☐ PLUCK ☐☐☐ MOXIE ☐☐☐

Teaching Values—Reaching Kids
© The Learning Works, Inc.

Create a Courage Cartoon

On a separate sheet of paper, see how many examples you can list of everyday moral courage. Then select one of your examples and create a cartoon strip illustrating a situation where a boy or girl your age exhibits moral courage.

COBALT BLUE   CRIMSON RED

Physical Courage

Boy Saves Drowning Brother in Backyard Swimming Pool

Ten-Year-Old Julia Juarez Crosses Finish Line in Wheelchair

Teenager Rescues Neighborhood Child From Burning Home

Local Girl Makes Olympic Finals

The newspaper headlines above are all examples of physical courage. Physical courage can be defined as someone putting his or her own safety aside to risk helping someone in need. Physical courage is also pushing your own body and strength to the maximum and doing something physical that is very difficult for you. Physical courage can also be competing against yourself to accomplish a physical goal rather than competing against someone else. Think about the following questions and statements and write brief answers for each one.

- How does physical courage differ from moral courage?

_____

_____

_____

- Describe a time you faced a physical challenge and had to do something that was very difficult for you—something that took physical strength and courage.

_____

_____

_____

- If you could choose a great physical feat to accomplish during your lifetime, what would it be?

_____

_____

Resisting Peer Pressure

Most kids know right from wrong. They wouldn't destroy someone else's property, lie, steal, or cheat. But sometimes kids act differently when they're in a group and do things under pressure from their classmates or friends that they would never consider doing on their own. Think about your own experiences with peer pressure and answer the following questions on a separate piece of paper.

- How would you define peer pressure?

- Why does it take courage to resist peer pressure?

- Have your friends ever pressured you into doing something that you really didn't want to do? Describe the experience.

- How did you feel about yourself afterwards?

- Have you ever stood up to your friends and resisted peer pressure? Describe the experience.

- How did you feel about yourself afterwards?

- Why do kids sometimes forget the values they believe in to go along with the crowd?

- What are some of the consequences of going along with the crowd, breaking the rules, and getting into trouble at home? at school? in the community?

- Have you ever broken up a friendship because the other person was always getting into trouble and didn't have the same values as you?

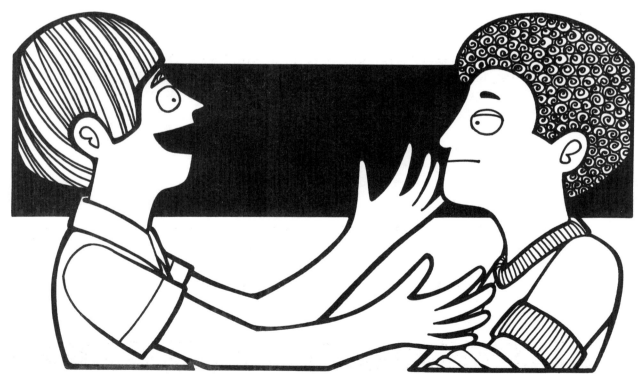

The Courage to Say "No"

It takes a lot of courage to say "no" and not go along with the crowd, especially if the crowd is a group of close friends or classmates. Sometimes you have to make difficult decisions on the spot as situations arise. Think about times you've responded hastily to a situation and made a poor decision because you didn't have time to think the consequences through clearly. You certainly can't be prepared for all situations that are going to come your way; but if you stop to think about how you would handle yourself in tough situations before these situations arise, you'll make wiser decisions if and when they actually do occur.

Here are some situations you might find yourself in. Discuss with your classmates ways to show courage and resist going along with the crowd in each situation. Think about the possible consequences of going along with the crowd. Share your ideas and talk about creative responses you could give in each case to resist peer pressure and maintain your self-respect.

- Kids are smoking marijuana at a party. The joint is passed to you.

- At a slumber party, a group of kids ask you to join them and sneak out to prowl around the neighborhood after midnight.

- Classmates dare you to drink a bottle of beer at a party.

- While at the mall, your friends decide it would be fun to each shoplift a CD from a store. They want you to help them.

- At recess, a classmate asks you to join her in giving a new kid in your class a hard time just because she is from another country.

With your classmates, make up other situations that involve peer pressure. For each one you list, decide on a course of action you could take if the situation actually happened. Then make a class poster that emphasizes the importance of showing courage when it comes to resisting peer pressure.

Teaching Values—Reaching Kids
© The Learning Works, Inc.

Courage at School

Being courageous means feeling strongly about something and acting on it, even if you're the only one who feels that way. It means being willing to take risks and stand up for your beliefs.

Here are some examples of situations in which kids showed courage at school.

Matthew has trouble with math. Even though he tries hard, he still doesn't understand it. He goes to his teacher and admits he needs additional help or a tutor after class to help him catch up.

At recess, Yolanda sees two girls teasing a boy who is wearing a hearing aid. She approaches the girls and tells them to stop making fun of the boy.

Samantha cheated during a test and feels guilty about it. The next day, she stays after class to talk to her teacher. Samantha admits she cheated and apologizes to her teacher.

What are some acts of courage you have seen at your school?

_____

_____

_____

_____

_____

_____

Courage in Social Situations

It's not always easy to speak out when you're hurt and upset with close friends or when something bad happens. It takes courage to confront another person, even a best friend, to work out differences and to solve problems. Write a brief answer describing what you would do in each of these social situations.

Your best friend joins a soccer team, but since you're not very athletic, you don't. Now she ignores you and chooses to spend time and do things only with members of the team.

You borrow a friend's bike because yours is being fixed. While you are inside a video store, someone steals your friend's bike. Your friend uses his bike to get to school each day.

At a classmate's birthday party, you overhear some kids giving a girl a hard time because she speaks with a foreign accent. They also begin telling jokes that make fun of her country.

While on a field trip, you see a student switching price tags in a museum gift shop on her way to the cash register. No one else has seen what she has done.

It Takes Courage

There are many situations in life that take a great deal of courage to handle. Each person handles things differently, but we can all learn from each other. Listed below are situations that are painful and hard to deal with. Go through the list and discuss each one with your classmates. Discuss who you could turn to for assistance and advice. Talk about steps you could take that would offer some comfort or help.

- In the middle of the school year you and your family move to another state.

- Your dad or mom loses his or her job.

- Someone you care about is abusing drugs or alcohol.

- You find out you have to have an operation.

- Your home and all your possessions are lost in a fire, flood, hurricane, or tornado.

- Your family pet is very sick, and the vet suggests putting her to sleep.

- Someone you love becomes seriously ill.

- Your grandmother or grandfather dies.

People of Courage

Listed below are the names of a few men and women of courage. How many do you recognize? Do you know why each of these people are famous and in what ways they were courageous?

Pick one of these men or women or select another outstanding person. Do research and write a one-page report about this person's acts of courage and contributions to society. Then, on a separate piece of white art paper, draw a picture of the man or woman you selected. Paste your report and illustration on a sheet of colored construction paper. Bind this page into a class scrapbook entitled "People of Courage."

Women

Jane Addams
Susan B. Anthony
Clara Barton
Mary McLeod Bethune
Elizabeth Blackwell
Pearl S. Buck
Marie Curie
Amelia Earhart
Anne Frank
Helen Keller
Clare Boothe Luce
Shannon Lucid
Hattie McDaniel
Margaret Mead
Golda Meir
Rosa Parks
Sally Ride
Eleanor Roosevelt
Florence Seibert
Maria Tallchief
Harriet Tubman
Mildred (Babe) Didrikson Zaharias

Men

Benjamin Banneker
Daniel Boone
Michael Chang
Albert Einstein
Medgar W. Evers
Galileo Galilei
Mahatma Gandhi
John H. Glenn, Jr.
Daniel K. Inouye
John F. Kennedy
Martin Luther King, Jr.
Abraham Lincoln
Isaac Newton
Paul Revere
Jonas Edward Salk
Albert Schweitzer
Henry David Thoreau
Charles E. Yeager
George Washington
Ryan White
Orville Wright
Wilbur Wright

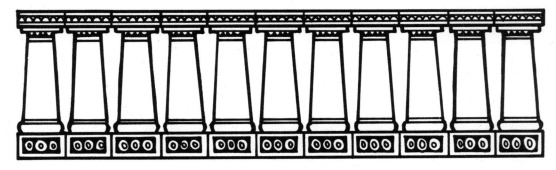

Take a Survey

Who are the men and women kids your age admire most when it comes to courage? Are these people political figures, movie stars, sports heroes, scientists, educators, or family members? Take a survey to find out by following these simple steps:

1. Brainstorm the names of women and men to place on your list of "People With Courage." They can be people from the past or the present. They can be people you know or people you've read about in newspapers or magazines. Make a list of these men and women and add their names to your list of "People With Courage."

2. Decide which classes in your school you plan to survey. You might start by just surveying other classes the same grade level as yours or expand the survey to include all the upper grades or all the primary grades. If you're really ambitious, take a survey of the entire student body.

3. Decide on the wording of your survey. How will you define courage for the kids participating in the survey?

4. Write a rough draft of your courage survey. Check it for clarity. Correct any spelling or punctuation errors, and then write your final draft.

5. Make copies of your final survey and conduct your survey asking students to select the five men and women they most admire for courage.

6. Analyze the results of your survey.

7. Share your findings and conclusions with your classmates and those who participated in the survey. Make a chart or poster to show the results.

PEOPLE WITH COURAGE SURVEY	MRS. ROBINSON'S CLASS PINE CREEK ELEMENTARY SCHOOL											
Martin Luther King, Jr.	X	X	X	X	X	X	X	X				
Helen Keller	X	X	X	X	X	X	X					
John Glenn	X	X	X	X	X							
Harriet Tubman	X	X	X	X	X	X						
Jackie Robinson	X	X	X	X	X							
Nathan Hale	X	X	X	X								
Winston Churchill	X	X	X									

Role-Playing Courage

Think about what you would do in each of the following situations. Then role-play the situation with several of your classmates. Show the rest of your class how you would solve each problem.

At school, at a party, or at camp, you walk into a room full of kids whom you have never met before. As you enter the room, they all turn and look at you.

You discover that an employee is stealing supplies from the company you work for. You decide to confront her before saying anything to the boss.

The school board is deciding whether students at your school should be required to wear uniforms. You are the only one in your class who is opposed to the idea. You decide to speak at the next board meeting to express your viewpoint.

Your dad drinks too much. He has lost his job several times because of his abuse of alcohol. At home he yells a lot and always seems angry. You finally get the courage to talk to someone about this problem.

Summing Up Courage

Complete each statement or question.

Something new I learned about courage is _____

_____

_____

_____

Did you reach the "courage" goals you set for yourself? Give examples of how you are moving toward them or have accomplished them.

_____

_____

_____

_____

_____

When it comes to courage:

- I think that I _____

- I was disappointed that I _____

- One change I want to make in myself is_____

    _____

One area I still need to work on when it comes to courage is_____

_____

_____

_____

_____

BRAVERY | VALOR | HEROISM

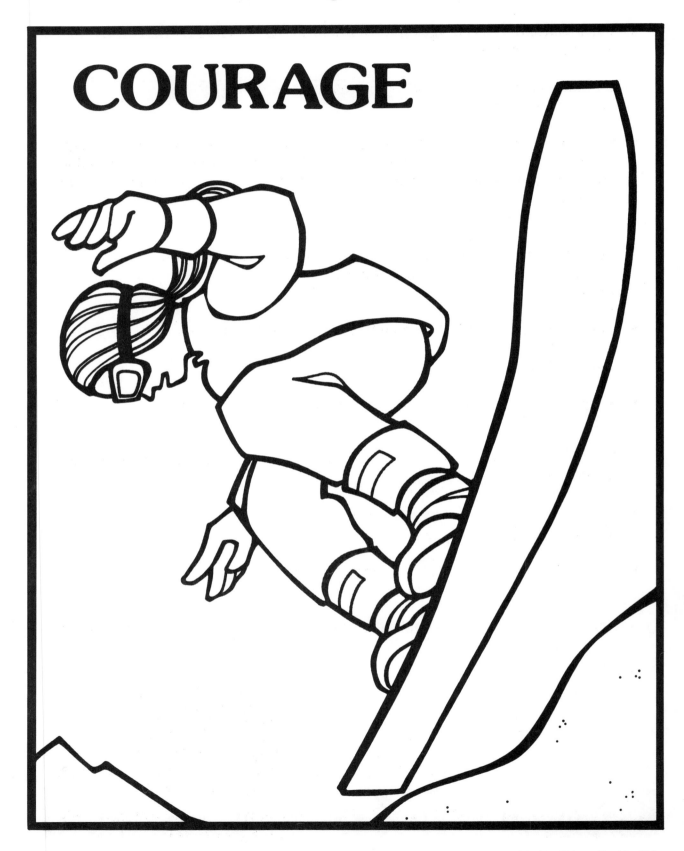

COURAGE

Quotes on Courage

- The greatest test of courage on earth is to bear defeat without losing heart.
  Robert Green Ingersoll

- I'd rather give my life than be afraid to give it.
  Lyndon Baines Johnson

- Far better is it to dare mighty things, to win glorious triumphs, even though checkered by failure, than to take rank with those poor spirits who neither enjoy much or suffer much, because they live in the grey twilight that knows not victory nor defeat.
  Theodore Roosevelt

- Courage is the price that life extracts for granting peace. The soul that knows it not, knows no release from little things.
  Amelia Earhart

- Courage is the first of human qualities because it is the quality which guarantees all the others.
  Winston Churchill

- Keep your fears to yourself, but share your courage with others.
  Robert Louis Stevenson

- The hero is no braver than an ordinary man, but he is brave five minutes longer.
  Ralph Waldo Emerson

- It is easy to be brave from a safe distance.
  from an Aesop fable

- Courage is the thing. All goes if courage goes.
  J. M. Barrie

- There is a strength of quiet endurance as significant of courage as the most daring feats of power.
  Henry Theodore Tuckerman

Quotes on Courage

- Sometimes even to live is an act of courage.
  Seneca

- Valor is a gift. Those having it never know for sure whether they have it till the test comes. And those having it in one test never know for sure if they will have it when the next test comes.
  Carl Sandburg

- Without justice, courage is weak.
  Benjamin Franklin

- No one can answer for his courage when he has never been in danger.
  La Rochefoucauld

- Life only demands from you the strength you possess. Only one feat is possible—not to have run away.
  Dag Hammarskjold

- It is courage, courage, courage, that raises the blood of life to crimson splendor.
  George Bernard Shaw

- Hidden valor is as bad as cowardice.
  Latin proverb

- Courage is resistance to fear, mastery of fear—not absence of fear.
  Mark Twain

- Perfect valor consists in doing without witness that which we would be capable of doing before everyone.
  La Rochefoucauld

Student Follow-Up Activities
Courage

- Do research about the life of a man or woman with a physical disability. Read to learn how he or she overcame great obstacles to achieve something special during his or her lifetime. Share your findings with your classmates.

- Plan a "Spotlight on Courage Week." Look for everyday acts of courage among your classmates and nominate these people to be in the spotlight. During the month you and your classmates are learning about courage, plan a program each Friday afternoon to recognize your peers who have done something courageous. Design an award or certificate to present to them. Post their pictures and a brief description of their courageous acts on a school bulletin board for other kids at your school to see.

Dog Rescues Owner from Burning House . . .
Horse Braves Storm to Carry Rider to Safety . . .

- Find stories in your local newspaper about pets and other animals who have shown great courage. Mount these stories on a classroom bulletin board.

- Write a poem about courage. The theme of your poem can be physical courage, emotional courage, or spiritual courage. Your poem does not have to rhyme.

- Find examples of courage in the books that your read throughout the school year. Your examples can come from your history books or from the literature you read. Make a poster to display in your classroom with the examples you discover..

- Get together with several of your classmates and plan a skit about courage. Write a script, rehearse your skit, and perform it for the rest of your class.

Teacher Follow-Up Activities
Courage

- Plan a "What If?" discussion in your classroom based on actual events in history. For example: What if Rosa Parks hadn't refused to give up her seat on a bus in Montgomery, Alabama? How might the course of history be different? Have students work with a partner to come up with an event in history that would make for a lively classroom discussion. The partners should do research on the background of the person or incident they have selected so they can answer questions from their peers.

- Invite guest speakers to your classroom to speak on courage. Police officers, fire fighters, probation officers, social workers, judges, doctors, nurses, and people from many other occupations have interesting stories they can share with your students.

- Use a small bulletin board in your classroom and create a "Courage Collage." Ask your students to contribute newspaper and magazine articles, pictures, photographs, and captions about courage to build the collage.

- Publish a classroom book about courage. Ask each student to write and illustrate an original, one-page essay, poem, or short story about courage. Combine all of the students' work to make a booklet to send home for parents to read.

- Brainstorm different types of courage as a culminating activity. Then ask your students to design and paint a classroom mural that captures the spirit of courage.

Chapter 8
Tolerance

**patience; open-mindedness;
sympathy for beliefs differing
from one's own**

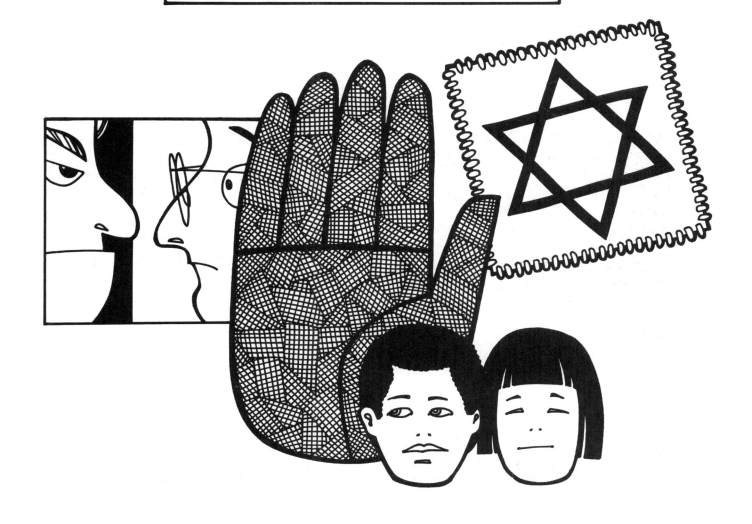

A Letter to Parents

Dear Parents,

This month our class will be learning about the value of **tolerance** through discussions, role-playing, creative writing, and art projects. We will learn about tolerance at school, at home, and for people in the community, and why tolerance is so important. We will learn about prejudice and about stereotyping people. We'll learn techniques for getting along with people whose ideas and viewpoints are different from our own.

Whenever possible, take time to talk to your child about tolerance. Discuss incidents from your own childhood that relate to tolerance. Describe how you felt when others were not understanding or tolerant of you. Invite your child to talk about things that have happened at school that have made him or her feel left out or discriminated against. Help your child to have empathy and concern for others by teaching him or her to always consider how another person might feel.

Here are other ways you can reinforce the value of tolerance with your child:

- Read the daily newspaper together as a family. Look for articles dealing with tolerance or the lack of tolerance. Use these articles as springboards for discussions and learning about tolerance. Allow everyone in your family to voice their opinions and feelings.

- As a family, read books that explore the value of tolerance. Ask your librarian to suggest novels that have tolerance as a theme, such as *The Diary of Anne Frank* or other books appropriate to the reading level of your child.

- In your child's school, there are probably children with many different cultural backgrounds. As a family, take time to learn about these cultures. Get books from the library and read about their holidays and celebrations. Help promote a better understanding of and appreciation for a wide variety of backgrounds. Talk about the similarities to your family's background as well as the differences from your culture.

Thank you for being our partner in helping to teach your child about the value of **tolerance**. Please feel free to visit our class and see what we're doing to learn more about tolerance and the understanding of beliefs that are different from our own.

Sincerely,

204

What is Tolerance?

In your own words, describe what the word *tolerance* means.

_____

_____

_____

_____

Find the word *tolerance* in a dictionary and write its definition below.

_____

_____

_____

_____

Describe a time when you were tolerant of another person's beliefs.

_____

_____

_____

_____

Describe a time when you were not tolerant of another person or of his or her beliefs.

_____

_____

_____

_____

What Are Examples of Tolerance?

You are being tolerant when you . . .

- listen to and respect a classmate's views and opinions even though they differ from yours

- are friends with people of different cultures

- can wait in long lines and keep your cool

- show understanding for kids in your class who are slower learners

- can get along with your classmates and treat them with respect

- take time to get to know what a person is really like and look beyond physical differences

- avoid stereotyping people and, instead, treat them as individuals

What other examples of tolerance can you list?

Setting Goals for Yourself

Set goals for yourself that involve tolerance. List one goal under each heading below. Think about how you can accomplish each goal. Take time to evaluate your goals on a regular basis to see how you're doing.

Tolerance at Home

Tolerance at School

Tolerance in Social Situations and/or in Sports

Tolerance for People in My Neighborhood and Community

What is Your Conscience?

When faced with a moral decision between doing right and wrong, why do some people make a good choice and others make a bad choice? How can some people purposely cause terrible harm to others and not be bothered by their acts? What does a person's conscience have to do with it? Answer the following questions on a separate piece of paper.

- What does the word *conscience* mean to you?

- Do you think all people have a conscience? Explain your answer.

- How, when, and where do you think people form a conscience?

- Describe a time you listened to your conscience.

- Describe a time you didn't listen to your conscience.

- How do you think your conscience helps you make decisions when it comes to values and morals?

208

Thoughts on Tolerance

Here are some questions to get you thinking about tolerance. Use them as topics for classroom discussions or answer them briefly on a separate piece of paper.

- In what ways are people throughout the world alike or similar?

- What basic needs do all people have?

- In what ways are people different?

- What technologies and inventions have brought people around the world closer together?

- Why do you think some people are intolerant of people who have skin color, religious beliefs, or political views that differ from their own?

- Why is it important to be tolerant of other people?

- Do you think tolerance of other people is something you are born with or a value you learn?

- In what ways does it take courage to be a tolerant person?

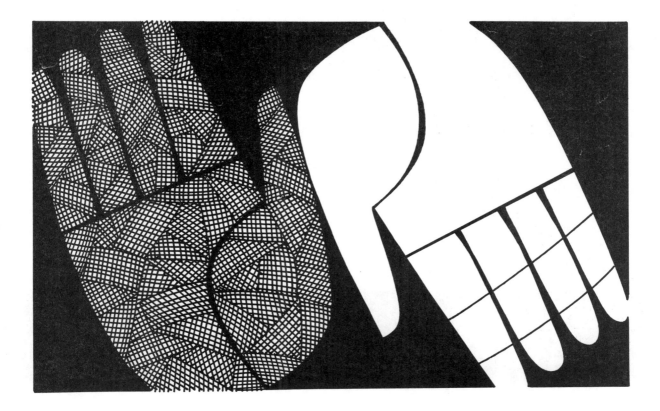

What Is a Prejudice?

A *prejudice* is a negative attitude toward a group of people who share some common characteristic. A prejudice is an opinion or judgment usually formed without proper knowledge or background. It is a hostile attitude that can be directed toward an individual, a group, or a race. People can be prejudiced against men or women; against people with black, white, brown, or yellow skin tones; against people who are Catholic, Jewish, Islamic, or Hindu; against people who are rich or poor, sick or disabled, tall or short, thin or fat.

Many times a person is prejudiced simply because he or she lacks knowledge about another person or group of people. He or she is quick to form an opinion about someone without taking the interest or time to really get to know him or her. Many times opinions of other people are based on *stereotypes*, or beliefs that all members of a certain group of people act in the same way.

On a separate piece of paper, describe a time you formed a hasty opinion of someone before you got to know him or her. In your description, answer the following questions:

- When did you first meet this person?

- Where and how did you meet?

- What was your first impression of this person?

- How did you get to know this person better?

- What interests did you discover you had in common?

- In what ways were you different?

- What is your relationship like today?

- What did you learn from this experience?

- How has this experience changed the way you form opinions about and treat people you have just met?

Tolerance for Other People

How tolerant of other people are you? Check "yes" or "no" to the following questions:

	YES	NO
1. Do you have a close friend who is of a different race than you?		
2. Do you have a close friend who is of a different religion than you?		
3. Are you usually patient with people who are physically and/or mentally disabled?		
4. Do you treat other people with respect, even those with whom you disagree?		
5. Do you try to compromise on issues instead of always insisting on having things your way?		
6. Do you avoid making stereotyped remarks about others?		
7. Do you try to be free of prejudices?		
8. When solving problems, to you try to find solutions that are fair to all sides?		
9. When you have a difference of opinion with someone, do you listen to his or her side with an open mind?		
10. Do you stand up for others and come to their defense when you see people treating them with intolerance?		

Complete the following statements:

• When it comes to being tolerant of other people, I think that I _____

_____

• I was surprised to learn that I _____

_____

• I could be more tolerant of _____

_____

Tolerance at Home

Living together as a family is not always easy. When you put people who have different personalities, viewpoints, and temperaments together under one roof, there are bound to be times when not everyone agrees and gets along. When disagreements arise at home, showing a little tolerance will go a long way. Here are some steps you can try to resolve differences at home and become a more tolerant person:

- Try putting yourself in the other person's shoes and seeing his or her side of the issue.

- Try being more patient and understanding.

- Try to reach a compromise where each person gives in a little.

- When there are disagreements in your family, talk about how you feel.

- If you are upset during a disagreement, tell the other person you need time to calm down, and schedule a time to talk about the problem after things have settled down a bit.

For each situation below, step into the underlined person's shoes and on a separate piece of paper, write his or her viewpoint. Then describe a compromise that could be reached to solve the problem.

- Your <u>sister</u> monopolizes the bathroom in the morning when you're trying to get ready for school.

- When your grandmother comes for her yearly visits, your <u>mom</u> hardly spends any time with you. You feel ignored and hurt.

- You share a bedroom with your younger <u>brother</u>. He doesn't respect your privacy and is always going through your belongings.

Write about a situation you have experienced involving tolerance at home. Describe what happened and how you resolved the problem.

Teaching Values—Reaching Kids
© The Learning Works, Inc.

Tolerance at School

What is a tolerant person? What qualities does he or she possess?

1. A tolerant person treats everyone with respect.

2. A tolerant person is accepting of people who are different from him or her and is open to differences of opinions, viewpoints, and beliefs.

4. A tolerant person seeks things in common with other people, not differences.

5. A tolerant person reaches out and learns from others.

6. A tolerant person is patient and understanding of others, regardless of the color of their skin, their religion, their age, or their appearance.

Describe a situation in which a classmate or friend was intolerant:

- of a fellow student,

- of a teacher,

- on the playground,

- in the cafeteria,

- during a game,

- while working on a class project in a small group, or

- of a substitute or visiting teacher

On a separate piece of paper, describe the events that led up to the incident. Describe what happened and what you learned about tolerance from this incident.

In Your Own Words

The following words about tolerance were written by American industrialist and politician Wendell L. Wilkie (1892–1944):

"Our way of living together in America is a strong but delicate fabric. It is made up of many threads. It has been woven over many centuries by the patience and sacrifice of countless liberty-loving men and women. It serves as a cloak for the protection of poor and rich, of black and white, of Jew and Gentile, of foreign and native born. Let us not tear it asunder. For no man knows, once it is destroyed, where or when man will find its protective warmth again."

Pretend you have been asked by your local newspaper to write your opinion about tolerance in the world today.

On a separate piece of paper, write a paragraph of no more than one hundred words, expressing your viewpoint and feelings about tolerance.

Role-playing Tolerance

Think about what you would do in each of the following situations. Then role-play the situation with several of your classmates. Show the rest of your class how you would solve each problem.

A teenager in your neighborhood is considered weird by your classmates because she has a pierced nose, dresses only in black, and has a tattoo. No one has made the effort to get to know her as a person. They are judging her only by her looks. You discover that she has had a hard life and comes from an abusive family. You decide to make an attempt to get to know her. Show how your efforts to be more tolerant change the attitudes of your classmates.

Jordan is confined to a wheelchair but doesn't let that stop him from doing anything. He's well liked by his classmates and is an excellent student. The trouble is that some older kids at school give him a hard time during recess. They tease him and make fun of him. You and a few of your friends decide to teach the older kids a much-needed lesson in tolerance. Decide how you would approach the older kids and what you would say and do.

People of Tolerance

To the Teacher:
- Divide your class into groups of four to five students per team.
- Reproduce the following list of questions for each group.
- Brainstorm with your students and ask them to list famous men and women of tolerance such as Martin Luther King, Jr.; Mother Teresa; and Mahatma Ghandi. Write these names on index cards, one name per card.
- Ask a member of each group to pick a different name. (The person selected becomes the focal point of their study.)
- Group members then work cooperatively to research and answer the questions based on the life of the person they selected. Each group presents their findings to the class when the research is completed.

Questions to Answer About People of Tolerance

Name of person selected _____

Group members _____

1. How would you describe this person's childhood?
2. What events in his or her life helped shape the person he or she became?
3. What were the political, social, and economic conditions that influenced this person's life?
4. What ten fascinating facts did you learned about this person from your research?
5. What special things did this person accomplish in his or her lifetime?
6. What difficulties did she or he have to overcome?
7. What events made this person become more tolerant?
8. If you could interview the person, what three questions would you ask him or her? What do you think his or her answers would be?
9. In what ways did this person of tolerance influence the world?
10. If you had to pick a man or woman living today who was most like the person you selected, who would it be? Why? In what ways are they similar? In what ways are they different?

Evaluation: What common traits did the class find among each of the women and men of tolerance?

216

Tolerance and Intolerance in History

Adolf Hitler came to power in Germany in 1933. He believed in a "master race" made up of a superior Aryan race of Nordic, blue-eyed, blond, light-skinned people. He tried to destroy minority races because he felt they were inferior. More than ten million Jews and people of other minority groups were put to death in gas chambers throughout Germany and Poland in the 1930s and 1940s. Millions more were put in concentration camps and were enslaved, experimented on, and tortured.

During this terrible time, many men and women risked their lives to hide Jewish children and families in their homes and save them from the Nazis death camps. Others made false passports to help Jews escape to countries such as Switzerland, Spain, and Sweden.

Do research to learn more about the Holocaust and examples of both tolerance and intolerance towards people during this period of history. Read about Anne Frank, a young girl who died in the concentration camps; Raoul Wallenberg, a Swedish businessman who sheltered and protected thousands of Hungarian Jews; and other notable men and women whose lives were affected by man's inhumanity to man.

In addition to reading books and reference materials in your library, you can also get information from several Internet sites:

The Museum of Tolerance
http://www.wiesenthal.com/mot/index.html

This site concentrates on human behavior, and the effects, historically, of a complete lack of social tolerance. An on-line museum tour is available, describing in detail each exhibit and its function. The Tolerancenter is a workshop discussing how persuasive people and media images influence our opinions and attitudes. The site also features a time line of the events leading up to and beyond the Los Angeles riots. The Holocaust Section explores the tragedy of Nazi Germany's attempt at genocide. The tour begins in pre-WWII Berlin, and explores not only the Holocaust, but the people of Germany, their culture, and their concerns over Nazi control of the state. This site also features biographies of Children of the Holocaust. These biographies, which change on a daily basis, present personal and detailed accounts of young Jews and their families.

United States Holocaust Memorial and Museum
http://www.ushmm.org/

Here, visitors can find an extensive database of resources and information on the victims and survivors of the Holocaust. Information on Anne Frank and Janusz Korczak, specifically, is also available, as well as information on camps, rescue efforts, the Resistance, U.S. and Allied responses, liberation, and post-Holocaust Germany. Visitors can also find information on the museum itself, hours of operation, group visits, directions, and membership information.

Internet Activities on Tolerance

Student's Forum for Studying the Holocaust
http://remember.org/imagine/index.html
This Web site includes "The Diary of Hannah Rosen: Europe's Jews and America's Response," a historical paper compiled from interviews with Jewish refugees in America during the war. A collection of children's art on the Holocaust is also featured, and children are invited to share their visual interpretations of the Holocaust with others on the site.

Kids4Peace
http://kids4peace.com/
Here, children are invited to play a part in "One Day of Peace," scheduled for January 1, 2000. They can perform the "One Day of Peace" play or download "We Can Work It Out" coloring pages. Children can visit the "Get Your Angries Out" page, and learn to control the Angries and resolve tough situations without hurting anyone's feelings. Children can also find "Peace Pals," and make new friends across the globe.

Here are some questions for you and your classmates to discuss:

1. What are some important lessons that can be learned about tolerance from the Holocaust?

2. Would you be willing to risk your own family's safety to help save another person's life?

3. Have you ever done anything to help overcome religious, racial, political, or gender intolerance at school or in your community? If so, explain what you did and the outcome of your actions.

4. Do you think there could ever be another Holocaust? Why or why not?

218

Summing Up Tolerance

Complete each statement or question.

Something new I learned about tolerance is _____

_____

_____

Did you reach the "tolerance" goals you set for yourself? Give examples of how you are moving toward them or have accomplished them.

_____

_____

_____

_____

_____

When it comes to tolerance:

• I think that I _____

_____

• I was disappointed that I _____

_____

• One change I want to make in myself is_____

_____

• One area I still need to work on is_____

_____

TOLERANCE

Quotes on Tolerance

- If you will please people, you must please them in their own way; and as you cannot make them what they should be, you must take them as they are.
  Lord Chesterfield

- It is a good thing to demand liberty for ourselves and for those who agree with us, but it is a better thing and a rarer thing to give liberty to others who do not agree with us.
  Franklin Delano Roosevelt

- If we cannot end our differences, at least we can help make the world a safer place for diversity.
  John Fitzgerald Kennedy

- Laws alone cannot secure freedom of expression; in order that every man present his views without penalty there must be a spirit of tolerance in the entire population.
  Albert Einstein

- Tolerance implies no lack of commitment to one's own beliefs. Rather it condemns the oppression or persecution of others.
  John Fitzgerald Kennedy

- The highest result of education is tolerance.
  Helen Keller

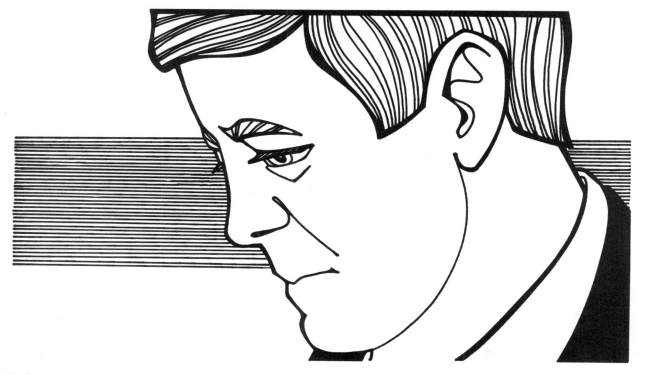

Student Follow-Up Activities
Tolerance

- Write a poem about tolerance. Use the letters in the word *tolerance* to begin each line of your poem. Try to capture the meaning and feeling of the word in your poem.

Example:

Trying to put yourself in another person's place

Opening your mind to new ideas and perspectives

Listening carefully to others

Endurance and patience

Reaching out to people who are different from you

Accepting them for who they are

Never being cruel or hurtful

Caring and showing compassion to the less fortunate

Ending fear and hating to create a world of peace and harmony

- Design a poster to display at school that teaches other kids about tolerance. Use words, pictures, and drawings to convey your message.

- Working with your classmates, select an incident that might actually happen in which a student is intolerant of another student at school. Then write a skit about this incident. Describe the events that lead up to a confrontation. In your skit, show how the incident is successfully resolved. Practice your skit and perform it for the other students in your class. Afterwards, lead the class in a discussion about what lesson is learned about tolerance through your skit.

- In your local newspaper, read and find articles dealing with tolerance. Try to find articles that show both tolerance towards others as well as articles that reflect intolerance. Use these articles as the focal point for class discussions and debates. You can also search the Internet for articles about tolerance and share them with your classmates.

Teaching Values—Reaching Kids
© The Learning Works, Inc.

Teacher Follow-Up Activities
Tolerance

- As a follow-up to a discussion of the Holocaust, ask your students to read a biography of Anne Frank or the book, *The Diary of Anne Frank*. Instead of writing a book report, ask students to share what they learned about tolerance after reading the book they selected. Encourage class discussions where students can answer questions such as:

  - In what ways was Anne Frank's life similar to yours? In what ways was it different?

  - Who were the people that helped Anne and her family?

  - Would you have been willing to protect Anne even if it meant death to your own family members if you were caught?

  - What can people do today to prevent anything like this from happening in the future?

  - Did reading the book you selected change your viewpoints on tolerance? If so, in what ways?

- Invite a Holocaust survivor from your community to speak to your students. (Contact the rabbi of your local synagogue for the names of people willing to speak to young people about their experiences.)

- Set aside a "Tolerance Week" in your classroom. During this time, ask your students to go out of their way to be especially tolerant of people in their families, of their peers at school, and of citizens in their community. After "Tolerance Week," ask students to share the results of their efforts and how people reacted. Discuss how they felt about the experience and what they learned about tolerance.

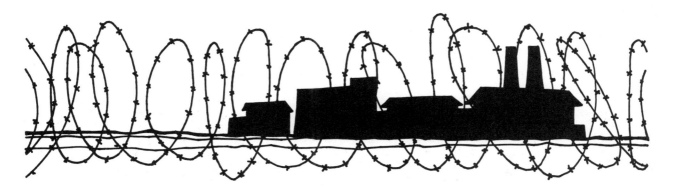

You Can Make a Difference

The world can be a scary place
Filled with hate and crime.
But you can make a difference,
If you'll just take the time,
To treat your friends and neighbors
With **tolerance** and **respect,**
And with **honesty** and kindness
In the ways *you* would expect.

Have **compassion** for others,
Let them know you care,
Try to right the wrongs you see
Cooperate and share.

Stick to goals you want to reach
Learn how to **persevere,**
Give every task your very best,
Let **courage** conquer fear.

Take **responsibility**
For all the things you do,
Don't put the blame on others,
Just be a friend that's true.

Yes, you can make a difference,
Put these values into play,
And try to do one special thing
For someone else each day.

If everybody did this,
There would be no wars or hate,
Instead—a world of love and peace,
Now, wouldn't that be great?

—*Linda Schwartz*

Write to us and tell us how you enjoyed the activities in *Teaching Values—Reaching Kids*. We'd love to hear from you! You can reach us at:

The Learning Works, Inc.
P.O. Box 6187
Santa Barbara, CA 93160